George Gascoigne:
edited by R(

G000240923

Also by Ronald Binns
Malcolm Lowry
"Perhaps the best short i̶n̶t̶r̶o̶d̶u̶c̶t̶i̶o̶n̶ ̶t̶o̶ ̶o̶n̶e̶ ̶o̶f̶ ̶t̶h̶e̶
neglected important writers of this century. For the
seasoned Lowryan, Binns's book is also important,
providing insights into the cultural and historical contexts
out of which the books themselves could emerge."
Philological Quarterly

"Develops fresh ideas and formulations. Binns has a
beautifully apposite quotation from Sartre, writes about
textual de-familiarisation in Lowry, about the collage-like
appearance of the writing, and has interesting points to
make about Trotksy, Joyce and Hardy in connection with
Under the Volcano."
Michael Hofmann, *Times Literary Supplement*

"With the general but astute reader always in mind, Binns
rights the topsy-turvy world of *Under the Volcano* chapter
by chapter and illuminates intelligently and
comprehensively the phantasmagori that crowd its
landscape"
American Library Association Booklist

"The best brief book on Malcolm Lowry"
Malcolm Bradbury, *Dangerous Pilgrimages* (1996)

J. G. Farrell
"Ronald Binns's excellent short study did much to keep
Farrell's reputation alive during the critical eclipse his
work suffered during the 1980s"
Ralph J. Crane, University of Waikato, New Zealand

George Gascoigne

Selected Poems

with 'Certayne notes of Instruction concerning the making of verse or ryme in English'

Edited, with an Introduction and Notes, by Ronald Binns

ZOILUS PRESS

First published in 2000 by Zoilus Press

Revised text, selection, introduction and notes
Copyright (c) Ronald Binns 2000

Ronald Binns is hereby identified as editor of this work
and has has asserted his rights in accordance with the
Copyright, Designs and Patents Act 1988

A CIP record for this book is available from the British
Library

Typeset by Electrograd

Printed and bound in Great Britain by Antony Rowe Ltd
Chippenham, Wiltshire

The cover reproduces the only contemporary portrait of
George Gascoigne, printed at the back of the title in the
original 1576 edition of *The Steele Glas.*

Zoilus Press, PO Box 9315, London E17 4UU

ISBN 1 902878 59 0

Introduction

This edition of George Gascoigne's poetry is intended to fill a glaring gap in contemporary publishing. At the start of the new millennium there is no selected or collected edition of Gascoigne's poems in print and none of his poetry is available in paperback, apart from one or two poems in anthologies.

Gascoigne published his first collection of writing in 1573, when he was probably in his mid-thirties. *A Hundreth sundrie Flowres* proved to be a controversial volume and was regarded in some quarters as scandalous and obscene. Apologising for the fact that its contents had been found to be "offensive for sundrie wanton speeches and lascivious phrases" and "doubtfully construed", Gascoigne produced a revised edition which was published two years later as *The Posies of George Gascoigne Esquire*. However although the contents were re-arranged he had changed very little and copies of the book were subsequently seized by the censors.

The Life of George Gascoigne

The only public building which today displays Gascoigne's name is the library at the junction of Wood Street and Forest Road in Walthamstow, London E17. Although nowadays this is a location which is heavily congested with traffic streaming in and out of London on the A503, the names of these streets testify to the rural past of the area. Two of the prefaces to *The Posies* end with the poet referring to "my poore house at Waltamstow [sic] in the Forest" and fragments of the once much more extensive Epping Forest remain dotted about the locality. Indeed, in one portion a mile or so to the north-east can be found Gascoigne Gardens, though the site of the poet's long-since demolished house is believed to lie in the vicinity of Thorpe Hall Road.

1

Carved in the wall of the library is the confident inscription GEORGE GASCOIGNE 1525-1577. We know that the second date is accurate, but the first is entirely speculative. Contemporary records suggest that the poet was born between 1537 and 1540. Gascoigne was therefore in his early twenties when he married and in his late thirties when he died.

George Gascoigne was born into the Tudor landed gentry, the first son of Sir John Gascoigne, a wealthy Bedfordshire landowner. He had some education in Westmoreland and later went to Cambridge University, but took no degree. In 1555 he was admitted to Gray's Inn as a law student. As a young man he followed in his father's footsteps and represented Bedford Borough in parliament. Gascoigne was present at the House of Commons for that dramatic moment on 17 November 1558 when news was brought of the death of Queen Mary and the succession of Elizabeth I. He participated in the coronation and attached himself to the court but seems to have experienced financial problems in sustaining an extravagant lifestyle. On 23 November 1561 he married Elizabeth Bretton, the wealthy widow of a London merchant, who owned properties in London and Walthamstow.

In the autumn of 1563 Gascoigne left the court and in the following years divided his time between properties in Bedfordshire (where he seems to have occupied himself with farming) and Walthamstow (where he apparently did his writing). In 1564 or 1565 he resumed his law studies at Gray's Inn, but never qualified and by 1567-1568 he was again in Bedfordshire. In 1570 Gascoigne was imprisoned for debt in Bedford prison. As his prospective careers as courtier and lawyer had both withered Gascoigne then tried soldiery. He went off twice to the Netherlands to fight on the side of the Dutch Protestant rebellion against the Spaniards, adopting as his motto *Tam Marti Quam Mercurio* ("Both for

Mars and for Mercury" - respectively the gods of war and eloquence). Eventually captured, Gascoigne was a prisoner of war for four months, before being freed and allowed to return to England in October 1574.

Although *A Hundreth sundrie Flowres* was offensive to powerful and censorious churchmen, there were others who evidently favoured Gascoigne's work. In 1575 the Earl of Leicester commissioned Gascoigne to write most of the entertainments provided for the Queen during her famous visit to Kenilworth, which apart from fireworks included masques, pageants and flattering verses and speeches. On the third day of the Queen's visit Gascoigne appeared before her, dressed up as a wild man of the woods, covered in moss and ivy. On another occasion Gascoigne dressed up again and ran along beside her horse, reciting verse at her. Later that year he was again involved in writing for the Queen's entertainment during her royal progress to Woodstock. This brief re-entry into the world of the court seems to have been beneficial and Gascoigne was subsequently employed by the government to visit the French court and the Low Countries and report back to Burghley and Walsingham. However by 1576 Gascoigne was in poor health and he died the following year.

Gascoigne the Writer

Gascoigne is nowadays remembered primarily as a lyric poet. He is often defined as the chief poet of the young Elizabeth's court and one of the greatest poets of the sixteenth century. Most of the love poems probably belong to the period when Gascoigne was a wealthy young man about town, hanging around the gilded world of the court, spending a small fortune on clothes, gambling and the pursuit of women. Strictly speaking, however, he was not a courtier at all, held no position at court and was probably excluded from the inner sanctum of the royal palaces. However, he did move in the wider world of the Tudor ruling class and his poetry was written for the entertainment of the educated, wealthy élite of contemporary London, whose lives and activities overlapped with those inside the privileged inner world of the court. Gascoigne was also a pioneering dramatist, translator, satirist and prose writer but apart from his short novel *The Adventures of Master F.J.* his other works nowadays remain largely unread, except by a small number of academic scholars.

Gascoigne's first publication, *A Hundreth sundrie Flowres*, seems to have been put together by the printer not quite in the way the author had wanted and its anonymity and the bogus addresses to the reader and letters of introduction suggest a nervous awareness on Gascoigne's part of its potentially offensive content. The volume consisted of two plays, a short, racy novel of adultery and one hundred poems. Whether or not it was banned is unclear but the book does seem to have caused a scandal. Two years later Gascoigne republished it under his own name with three prefaces claiming his work had been much misunderstood, together with a score of commendatory verses. As *The Posies of George Gascoigne Esquire* it included a bowdlerised version of the novel (which he now breezily presented as the translation of some Italian tales by the non-existent "Bartello") and a re-arranged presentation of the poems, few of which were significantly revised. Included for the first time was Gascoigne's pioneering essay on English prosody, "Certayne notes of Instruction concerning the making of verse or ryme in English." A year later fifty unsold copies of the *Posies* were seized by the church censors. This selection draws on both editions.

Gascoigne's versatility and originality is evident in his poems, which employ a variety of forms, have a wide metrical range and which include satires, tender love lyrics, complaints, narrative verse, elegies, religious meditations, riddles, verse autobiography and chatty conversational pieces. This rich, discordant clash of style and subject is mirrored in Gascoigne's own perception of himself as a divided personality - part warrior and man of action, part writer and man of bookish interests. Look in the background of the portrait of Gascoigne reproduced on the cover of this book and you can make out on one side a musket with pouches for powder and shot and on the other a bookshelf with books, pen and ink.

My selection of his verse is entirely personal but provides, I hope, a reasonably representative sample of Gascoigne's versatility as a poet, ranging from the lyric simplicity of his shorter love poems to the racy, conversational, knockabout satire of "Counsel given to master Bartholmew Withipoll" and the more reflective tone struck by "Gascoigne's Good Morrow" and "Gascoigne's Good Night".

Gascoigne's essay on prosody "Certayne notes of Instruction concerning the making of verse or ryme in English" was the first of its kind in English and belongs in the same tradition as (to give a striking twentieth century example) Vladimir Mayakovksy's *How are Verses Made?* Its central argument is that English poets should write in plain, simple, ordinary language. Meaning, for Gascoigne, always came first, and blunt, straightforward verse using plain diction is always to be preferred to ornate, obscure rhetoric which prizes colourful literary effect above sense. His remark that "the more monosyllables that you use, the truer Englishman you shall seem" is often quoted, though the advice seems faintly ironic, bearing in mind that it is given to an Italian. It would be a mistake to see Gascoigne as a crude, unsophisticated writer. His sense of rhythm and assonance is acute, and his fondness for alliteration (seen, for example, in the line "Catch, snatch, and scratch for scrapings and for crumbs") looks back to Chaucer and

5

Anglo-Saxon verse as well as sometimes seeming oddly akin to the style of Gerard Manley Hopkins.

Gascoigne solemnly warned that "to intermingle merry jests in a serious matter is an indecorum" but it must be noted that he was a master of the art of *double entendre* and some of the poems included here can be read innocently or indecently, according to the state of mind of the reader. For example, whether or not "The Praise of Phillip Sparrow" is simply about a bird or is an exercise in obscene innuendo, is a very open question (my own view is that it is a lively and even boastful celebration of the adventures of Gascoigne's penis). On the whole however it is true that his practice matched his theory and that his verse is characterized by a blunt, assertive diction which avoids baroque ornament. "And If I Did What Then?" shows Gascoigne at his most effective, expressing in clear forceful language the end of a love affair.

The influence of Petrarch is strong in some of the sonnets which were probably among Gascoigne's earliest work, and as Don Paterson comments in his excellent anthology *101 Sonnets* (London, 1999) the poet, like his contemporaries, sometimes fell victim to "superfluous couplet syndrome". But Gascoigne soon forged his own unique style of verse-making, ranging from the animated monologues addressed to friends and patrons to the moving and beautifully effective plain-style lyrics such as "Gascoigne's Good Morrow" and "The Lullaby of a Lover". Much of Gascoigne's subject matter seems autobiographical to a degree quite unusual for the time. "The Arraignment of a Lover" laconically draws on his legal training at Gray's Inn, while "Gascoigne's Woodmanship" playfully narrates his fruitless endeavours as a law student, courtier and soldier. The tone of the narrative poems is sometimes reminiscent of Byron's witty, risk-taking satire, especially *Don Juan*. The jesting, playful Gascoigne is again revealed in "Either a

6

Needless or a Bootless Comparison Between Two Letters", which toys with the contrast between 'B' (for Boyes, his wife's previous husband) and 'G' for Gascoigne.

The narrative poems, such as "Gascoigne's Voyage into Holland in 1572", require some knowledge of contemporary events and are effective as a kind of dramatic journalism in verse. "Gascoigne's De Profundis" seems to express a more thoughtful, meditative Gascoigne, though even here the poet speaks in a blunt, muscular no-nonsense kind of voice ("O gracious God, to thee I cry and yell"), climaxing with a thunderous last stanza.

Perhaps most basic of all in Gascoigne's poetry is a sense of the various failures of his life, and many of the poems turn on the idea of thwarted fate, frustrated desire and rejection. Nothing ever quite seemed to go right for Gascoigne, whether it was matters of finance or the heart, family life, his marriage, his career in law and as a soldier, or even at Kenilworth, where the oak sapling he was holding almost hit the Queen's horse, startling it, and where his specially written masque went unperformed because of bad weather. That his work has been out of print for many years (except in expensive and obscure editions) and that Walthamstow, the place where much of his writing was accomplished, has largely forgotten he ever existed, and remembers him with an inaccurately dated engraving on a wall passed by traffic but where few ever walk, would surely have seemed to Gascoigne all too apt.

Further Reading

George Gascoigne (ed. with an Introduction and Notes by C.T. Prouty) *A Hundreth sundrie Flowres* (Missouri, 1942)
Ronald C. Johnson, *George Gascoigne* (New York, 1972)
C.T. Prouty, *George Gascoigne: Elizabethan Courtier, Soldier and Poet* (New York, 1942)

A NOTE ON THE TEXT

No modern edition which is not a facsimile can possibly hope to reproduce the textual authenticity or feel of the original editions of Gascoigne's work. Gascoigne's writing was published in the sixteenth century, and any editor of his work is faced with a choice between reproducing the original text exactly, presenting a semi-modernised version of Elizabethan English or modernising it throughout.

I have opted for the middle possibility. On the whole I have modernised only words the spelling of which has changed but not the meaning. In this edition "poeme" becomes "poem"; "inough" becomes "enough"; "woordes" becomes "words", and so on. I have preferred not to modernise words which are now not in common use, or where the rhythm of Gascoigne's prose or poetry would have been significantly altered. Only very rarely have I modernised Gascoigne's syntax, which to twenty-first century eyes may appear idiosyncratic. I have omitted most of the repetitive Latin tags or "posies" which Gascoigne often used after individual poems. The only serious liberty I have taken with Gascoigne's poetry is occasionally to provide briefer titles, usually taken from the first line of the poem, in place of a sometimes lengthy introductory title.

ACKNOWLEDGEMENT

I am very grateful to James Binns for translating Latin used by Gascoigne and to him and Dr H. Neville Davies for helping me to understand the language and culture of Elizabethan England.

8

CONTENTS

Selected Poems

9

In Praise of the Brown Beauty

The thriftless thread which pampered beauty spins,
In thraldom binds the foolish gazing eyes:
As cruel spiders with their crafty ginnes,
In worthless webs do snare the simple flies.
The garments gay, the glittering golden gite,
The tysing talk which flows from Pallas pools:
The painted pale, the (too much) red made white,
Are smiling baits to fish for loving fools.
But lo, when eld in toothless mouth appears,
And hoary hairs instead of beauty's blaze:
Then had I wist, doth teach repenting years,
The tickle track of crafty Cupid's maze.
Twixt fair and foul therefore, twixt great and small,
A lovely nutbrown face is best of all.

When First I Thee Beheld

When first I thee beheld in colours black and white,
Thy face in form well framed with favour blooming still:
My burning breast in cares did choose his chief delight,
With pen to paint thy praise, contrary to my skill:
Whose worthiness compared with this my rude devise,
I blush and am abashed, this work to enterprise.

But when I call to mind thy sundry gifts of grace,
Full fraught with manners meek in happy quiet mind:
My hasty hand forthwith doth scribble on apace,
Lest willing heart might think, it meant to come behind:
Thus do both hand and heart these careful metres use,
Twixt hope and trembling fear, my duty to excuse.

Wherefore accept these lines, and banish dark disdain,
Be sure they come from one that loveth thee in chief:
And guerdon me thy friend in like with love again,
So shalt thou well be sure to yield me such relief,
As only may redress my sorrows and my smart:
For proof whereof I pledge (dear Dame) to thee my heart.

Her Question

What thing is that which swims in bliss,
And yet consumes in burning grief:
Which being placed where pleasure is,
Can yet recover no relief.
Which sees to sigh, and sighs to see,
All this is one, what may it be?

The Praise of Phillip Sparrow

Of all the birds that I do know,
Phillip my sparrow hath no peer:
For sit she high or lie she low,
Be she far off, or be she near,
There is no bird so fair, so fine,   5
Nor yet so fresh as this of mine.

Come in a morning merrily,
When Phillip hath been lately fed,
Or in an evening soberly,
When Phillip list to go to bed: 10
It is a heaven to hear my phippe,
How she can chirp with cherry lip.

She never wanders far abroad,
But is at hand when I do call:
If I command she lays on load,   15
With lips, with teeth, with tongue and all.
She chants, she chirps, she makes such cheer,
That I believe she hath no peer.

And yet besides all this good sport,
My Phillip can both sing and dance: 20
With newfound toys of sundry sort,
My Phillip can both prick and prance:
As if you say but fend cut phippe,
Lord how the peat will turn and skip.

Her feathers are so fresh of hue,   25
And so well proyned every day:
She lacks none oil, I warrant you:
To trim her tail both trick and gay,
And though her mouth be somewhat wide,

13

Her tongue is sweet and short beside. 30

And for the rest I dare compare,
She is both tender, sweet and soft:
She never lacketh dainty fare,
But is well fed and feedeth oft:
For if my phip have lust to eat, 35
I warrant you phip lacks no meat.

And then if that her meat be good,
And such as like do love alway:
She will lay lips thereon by-the-rood,
And see that none be cast away: 40
For when she once hath felt a fit,
Phillip will cry still, yit, yit, yit.

And to tell truth he were to blame,
Which had so fine a bird as she,
To make him all this goodly game, 45
Without suspect or jealousy:
He were a churl and knew no good,
Would see her faint for lack of food.

Wherefore I sing and ever shall,
To praise as I have often proved 50
There is no bird amongst them all,
So worthy for to be beloved.
Let others praise what bird they will,
Sweet Phillip shall be my bird still.

Soon Acquainted, Soon Forgotten

If what you want, you (wanton) had at will,
A steadfast mind, a faithful loving heart:
If what you speak you would perform it still,
If from your word your deed did not revert:
If youthful years your thoughts did not so rule,
As elder days may scorn your friendship frail,
Your doubled fancy would not thus recule,
For peevish pride which now I must bewail.
For Cresside fair did Troilus never love,
More dear than I esteemed your freamed cheare,
Whose wavering ways (since now I do them prove)
By true report this witness with me bear:
That if your friendship be not too dear bought,
The price is great, that nothing gives for nought.

A Riddle

A Lady once did ask of me,
This pretty thing in privitie:
Good sir (quod she) fain would I crave,
One thing which you yourself not have:
Nor never had yet in times past,
Nor never shall while life doth last.
And if you seek to find it out,
You lose your labour out of doubt:
Yet if you love me as you say,
Then give it me, for sure you may.

15

A Lover Often Warned

I that my race of youthful years had run
Always untied, and not (but once) in thrall,
Even I which had the fields of freedom won,
And lived at large, and played with pleasure's ball:
Lo now at last am tane again and taught,
To taste such sorrows, as I never sought.

I love, I love, alas I love indeed,
I cry alas, but no man pities me:
My wounds are wide, yet seem they not to bleed,
And hidden wounds are hardly held we see.
Such is my luck to catch a sudden clap,
Of great mischance in seeking my good hap.

My mourning mind which dwelt and died in dole,
Sought company for solace of the same:
My cares were cold, and craved comfort's coal,
To warm my will with flakes of friendly flame.
I sought and found, I craved and did obtain,
I won my wish, and yet I got no gain.

For whiles I sought the cheer of company,
Fair fellowship did wonted woes revive:
And craving medicine for my malady,
Dame pleasure's plaster proved a corrosive.
So that by mirth, I reaped no fruit but moan,
Much worse I fear, than when I was alone.

The cause is this, my lot did light too late,
The birds were flown before I found the nest:
The steed was stolen before I shut the gate,
The cates consumed, before I smelt the feast.
And I fond fool with empty hand must call,

The gorged hawk, which likes no lure at all.

Thus still I toil, to till the barren land,
And grope for grapes among the bramble briars:
I strive to sail and yet I stick on sand,
I deem to live, yet drown in deep desires.
These lots of love, are fit for wanton will,
Which finds too much, yet must be seeking still.

The Constancy of a Lover

That self same tongue which first did thee entreat
To link thy liking with my lucky love:
That trusty tongue must now these words repeat,
I love thee still, my fancy cannot move.
That dreadless heart which durst attempt the thought
To win thy will with mine for to consent,
Maintains that vow which love in me first wrought,
I love thee still, and never shall repent.
That happy hand which hardly did touch
Thy tender body to my deep delight:
Shall serve with sword to prove my passion such
As loves thee still, much more than it can write.
Thus love I still with tongue, hand, heart and all,
And when I change, let vengeance on me fall.

The Arraignment of a Lover

At Beauty's bar as I did stand,
When false suspect accused me,
George (quod the Judge) hold up thy hand,
Thou art arraigned of flattery:
Tell therefore how thou wilt be tried?
Whose judgement here wilt thou abide?

My Lord (quod I) this Lady here,
Whom I esteem above the rest,
Doth know my guilt if any were:
Wherefore her doom shall please me best,
Let her be judge and juror both,
To try me guiltless by mine oath.

Quod Beauty, no, it sitteth not,
A Prince herself to judge the cause:
Here is our justice well you wot,
Appointed to discuss our laws:
If you will guiltless seem to go,
God and your country quit you so.

Then craft the cryer called a quest,
Of whom was falsehood foremost fear,
A pack of pickethankes were the rest,
Which came false witness for to bear,
The jury such, the judge unjust,
Sentence was said I should be trussed.

Jealous the jailer bound me fast,
To hear the verdict of the bill,
George (quod the Judge) now thou art cast,
Thou must go hence to heavy hill,

And there be hanged all but the head,
God rest thy soul when thou art dead.

Down fell I then upon my knee,
All flat before Dame Beauty's face,
And cried, good Lady pardon me,
Which here appeal unto your grace,
You know if I have been untrue,
It was in too much praising you.

And though this judge do make such haste,
To shed with shame my guiltless blood:
Yet let your pity first be placed,
To save the man that meant you good,
So shall you show yourself a Queen,
And I may be your servant seen.

(Quod Beauty) well: because I guess,
What thou dost mean henceforth to be,
Although thy faults deserve no less,
Than justice here hath judged thee,
Wilt thou be bound to stint all strife,
And be true prisoner all thy life?

Yea Madame (quod I) that I shall,
Lo faith and truth my sureties:
Why then (quod she) come when I call,
I ask no better warranties.
Thus am I Beauty's bounden thrall,
At her command when she doth call.

Gascoigne's Passion

I smile sometimes although my grief be great,
To hear and see these lovers paint their pain,

And how they can in pleasant rhymes repeat,
The passing pangs, which they in fancies feign.
But if I had such skill to frame a verse
I could more pain than all their pangs rehearse.

Some say they find nor peace, nor power to fight,
Which seemeth strange: but stranger is my state:
I dwell in dole, yet sojourn with delight,
Reposed in rest, yet worried with debate.
For flat repulse, might well appease my will,
But fancy fights, to try my fortune still.

Some others say they hope, yet live in dread,
They freeze, they flame, they fly aloft, they fall,
But I nor hope with hap to raise my head,
Nor fear to stoop, for why my gate is small.
Nor can I freeze, with cold to kill my heart,
Nor yet so flame, as might consume my smart.

How live I then, which thus draw forth my days?
Or tell me how, I found this fever first?
What fits I feel? what distance? what delays?
What grief? what ease? what like I best? what worst?
These things they tell, which seek redress of pain,
And so will I, although I count it vain.

I live in love, even so I love to live,
(Oh happy state, twice happy he that finds it)
But love to life this cognisance doth give,
This badge this mark, to every man that minds it,
Love lendeth life, which (dying) cannot die,
Nor living live: and such a life lead I.

The sunny days which glad the saddest wights,
Yet never shine to clear my misty moon:

20

No quiet sleep, amid the moonshine nights,
Can close mine eyes, when I am woebegone.
Into such shades my peevish sorrow shrouds,
That sun and moon, are still to me in clouds.

And feverlike I feed my fancy still,
With such repast, as most impairs my health,
Which fever first I caught by wanton will,
When coals of kind did stir my blood by stealth:
And gazing eyes, in beauty put such trust
That love enflamed my liver all with lust.

My fits are like the fever Ectyck fits,
Which one day quakes within and burns without,
The next day heat within the bosoms sits,
And shivering cold the body goes about.
So is my heart most hot when hope is cold,
And quaketh most when I most heat behold.

Tormented thus without delays I stand,
Always in one and evermore shall be,
In greatest grief when help is nearest hand,
And best at ease if death might make me free:
Delighting most in that which hurts my heart,
And hating change which might relieve my smart.

Yet you dear dame: to whom this cure pertains,
Devise betimes some drams for my disease,
A noble name shall be your greatest gains,
Whereof be sure, if you will work mine ease.
And though fond fools set forth their fits as fast,
Yet grant with me that Gascoigne's passion past.

Ever or never.

21

A Hundreth Suns

A hundreth suns (in course but not in kind)
Can witness well that I possess no joy:
The fear of death which fretteth in my mind
Consumes my heart with dread of dark anoye.
And for each sun a thousand broken sleeps
Divide my dreams with fresh recourse of cares:
The youngest sister sharp her shear she keeps,
To cut my thread, and thus my life it wears.
Yet let such days, such thousand restless nights,
Spit forth their spite, let fates eke show their force:
Death's daunting dart where so his buffet lights,
Shall shape no change within my friendly corse:
But dead or live, in heaven, in earth, in hell
I will be thine where so my carcase dwell.

His Riddle

I cast mine eye and saw ten eyes at once,
All seemly set upon one lovely face:
Two gazed, two glanced, two watched for the nonce,
Two winked wiles, two frowned with forward grace.
Thus every eye was pitched in his place.
And every eye which wrought each other's woe,
Said to itself, alas why looked I so?
And every eye for jealousy did pine,
And sighed and said, I would that eye were mine.

Gascoigne's Libel of Divorce

Divorce me now good death, from love and lingering life,
That one hath been my concubine, that other was my wife.
In youth I lived with love, she had my lusty days,
In age I thought with lingering life to stay my wandering
ways,
But now abused by both, I come for to complain
To thee good death, in whom my help doth wholly now
remain,
My libel lo behold: wherein I do protest,
The process of my plaint is true, in which my grief doth rest.
First love my concubine, whom I have kept so trim,   9
Even she for whom I seemed of yore, in seas of joy to swim:
To whom I dare avow, that I have served as well,
And played my part as gallantly, as he that bears the bell:
She cast me off long since, and holds me in disdain,
I cannot prank to please her now, my vaunting is but vain.
My wrinkled cheeks betray, that pride of heat is past,
My staggering steps eke tell the truth, that nature fadeth fast.
My quaking crooked joints, are cumbered with the cramp,
The box of oil is wasted well, which once did feed my lamp.
The greenness of my years, doth wither now so sore,
That lusty love leaps quite away, and liketh me no more,   20
And love my lemman gone, what liking can I take?
In loathsome life that crooked crone, although she be my
make?
She cloys me with the cough, her comfort is but cold,
She bids me give mine age for alms, where first my youth
was sold.
No day can pass my head, but she begins to brawl,
No merry thoughts conceived so fast, but she confounds
them all.
When I pretend to please, she overthwarts me still,
When I would fainest part with her, she overways my will.

Be judge then gentle death, and take my cause in hand,
Consider every circumstance, mark how the case doth stand.
Percase thou wilt allege, that cause thou canst none see,
But that I like not of that one, that other likes not me:
Yes gentle judge give ear, and thou shalt see me prove,
My concubine incontinent, a common whore is love.
And in my wife I find, such discord and debate,
As no man living can endure the torments of my state.
Wherefore thy sentence say, divorce me from them both,
Since only thou mayst right my wrongs, good death now be
                                                    not loth.
But cast thy piercing dart, into my panting breast,
That I may leave both love and life, & thereby purchase rest.

You Must Not Wonder

You must not wonder though you think it strange,
To see me hold my louring head so low:
And that mine eyes take no delight to range,
About the gleams which on your face do grow.
The mouse which once hath broken out of trap,
Is seldom tysed with the trustless bait,
But lies aloof for fear of more mishap,
And feedeth still in doubt of deep deceit.
The scorched fly, which once hath 'scaped the flame,
Will hardly come to play again with fire:
Whereby I learn, that grievous is the game,
Which follows fancy dazzled by desire.
So that I wink, or else hold down my head,
Because your blazing eyes, my bale have bred.

24

Gascoigne's Recantation

Now must I needs recant the words which once I spoke,
Fond fancy fumes so nigh my nose, I needs must smell the
                                smoke:
And better were to bear a faggot from the fire,
Than wilfully to burn and blaze in flames of vain desire.
You judges then give ear, you people mark me well
I say, both heaven and earth record the tale which I shall tell
And know that dread of death, nor hope of better hap,
Have forced or persuaded me to take my turning cap,
But even that mighty Jove, of his great clemency,   9
Hath given me grace at last to judge, the truth from heresy:
I say then and profess, with free and faithful heart,
That women's vows are nothing else but snares of secret
                                smart:
Their beauty's blaze are baits which seem of pleasant taste,
But who devours the hidden hook, eats poison for repast:
Their smiling is deceit, their fair words trains of treason,
Their wit always so full of wiles, it scorneth rules of reason.
Percase some present here, have heard myself of yore,
Both teach and preach the contrary, my fault was then the
                                more:
I grant my works were these, first one *Anatomy*,
Wherein I painted every pang of love's perplexity: 20
Next that I was arraigned, with *George* hold up thy hand,
Wherein I yielded beauty's thrall, at her command to stand:
Mine eyes so blinded were, (good people mark my tale)
That once I sang, I *Bathe in Bliss*, amid my weary *Bale*:
And many a frantic verse, then from my pen did pass,
In waves of wicked heresy so deep I drowned was,
All which I now recant, and here before you burn
Those trifling books, from whose lewd lore my tippet here I
                                turn.
And henceforth will I write, how mad is that man's mind,

Which is enticed by any train to trust in womankind.   30
I spare not wedlock I, who list that state advance,
Ask *Astolf* king of *Lombardy*, how trim his dwarf could
                                                          dance.

Wherefore fair ladies you, that hear me what I say,
If you hereafter see me slip, or seem to go astray:
Or if my tongue revolt from that which now it sayth,
Then plague me thus, *believe it not*, for this is now my faith.

Either a Needless or a Bootless Comparison
Between Two Letters

Of all the letters in the christ's cross row,
 I fear (my sweet) thou lovest *B.* the best,
And though there be good letters many mo,
As *A. O. G. N. C. S.* and the rest,
Yet such a liking bearest thou to *B.*
That few or none thou thinkest like it be.

And much I muse what madness should thee move,
To set the cart before the comely horse:
Must *A.* give place to *B.* for his behove?
Are letters now so changed from their course?
Then must I learn (though much unto my pain),
To read (anew) my christ cross row again.

When first I learned, *A.* was in high degree,
A captain letter, and a vowel too:
Such one as was always a help to *B.*
And lent him sound and taught him what to do.
For take away the vowels from their place,
And how then can the consonants have grace?

Yet if you like a consonant so well,
Why should not *G.* seem better far than *B?*
G. spelleth God, that high in heaven doth dwell,
So spell we Gold and all good things with *G.*
B. serves to spell bald, bawdy, brain-sick, bold,
Black, brown and bad, yea worse than may be told.

In song, the *G.* clef keeps the highest place,
Where *B.* sounds always (or too sharp or) flat:
In *G. sol, re, ut,* trebles have trim grace.
B. serves the bass and is content with that.
Believe me (sweet) *G.* giveth sound full sweet,
When *B.* cries buzz, as is for basses meet.

But now percase thou wilt one *G.* permit,
And with that *G.* thou meanest *B.* to join:
Alas, alas, methinks it were not fit,
(To cloak thy fault) such fine excuse to coin.
Take double *G.* for thy most loving letter,
And cast off *B.* for it deserves no better.

Thus have I played a little with thy *B.*
Whereof the brand is thine, and mine the blame:
The wight who wounds thy wandering will is he,
And I the man that seek to salve thy name:
The which to think, doth make me sigh sometime,
Though thus I strive to jest it out in rhyme.

Gascoigne's Good Morrow

You that have spent the silent night,
In sleep and quiet rest,
And joy to see the cheerful light
That riseth in the East:
Now clear your voice, now cheer your heart,
Come help me now to sing:
Each willing wight come bear a part,
To praise the heavenly King.

And you whom care in prison keeps,
Or sickness doth suppress,
Or secret sorrow breaks your sleeps,
Or dolours do distress:
Yet bear a part in doleful wyse,
Yea think it good accord,
And acceptable sacrifice,
Each sprite to praise the Lord.

The dreadful night with darksomeness,
Had overspread the light,
And sluggish sleep with drowsiness,
Had overpressed our might:
A glass wherin we may behold,
Each storm that stops our breath,
Our bed the grave, our clothes like molde,
And sleep like dreadful death.

Yet as this deadly night did last,
But for a little space,
And heavenly day now night is past,
Doth show his pleasant face:
So must we hope to see God's face,
At last in heaven on high,

When we have changed this mortal place,
For immortality.

And of such haps and heavenly joys,
As then we hope to hold,
All earthly sights and worldly toys,
Are tokens to behold:
The day is like the day of doom,
The sun, the Son of man,
The skies the heavens, the earth the tomb
Wherein we rest till than.

The rainbow bending in the sky,
Bedecked with sundry hues,
Is like the seat of God on high,
And seems to tell these news:
That as thereby he promised,
To drown the world no more,
So by the blood which Christ hath shed,
He will our health restore.

The misty clouds that fall sometime,
And overcast the skies,
Are like to troubles of our time,
Which do but dim our eyes:
But as such dews are dried up quite,
When Phœbus shows his face,
So are such fancies put to flight,
Where God doth guide by grace.

The carrion crow, that loathsome beast,
Which cries against the rain,
Both for her hue and for the rest,
The Devil resembleth plain:
And as with guns we kill the crow,

For spoiling our relief,
The Devil so must we overthrow,
With gunshot of belief.

The little birds which sing so sweet,
Are like the angels' voice,
Which render God his praises meet,
And teach us to rejoice:
And as they more esteem that mirth,
Than dread the night's annoy,
So must we deem our days on earth,
But hell to heavenly joy.

Unto which joys for to attain
God grant us all his grace,
And send us after worldly pain,
In heaven to have a place.
Where we may still enjoy that light,
Which never shall decay:
Lord for thy mercy lend us might,
To see that joyful day.

Gascoigne's Good Night

When thou hast spent the lingering day in pleasure and
delight,
Or after toil and weary way, dost seek to rest at night:
Unto thy pains or pleasures past, add this one labour yet,
Ere sleep close up thine eye too fast, do not thy God forget,
But search within thy secret thoughts what deeds did thee
befall:
And if thou find amiss in ought, to God for mercy call:
Yea though thou find nothing amiss, which thou canst call to
mind,
Yet evermore remember this, there is the more behind:
And think how well so ever it be, that thou hast spent the
day,
It came of God, and not of thee, so to direct thy way.
Thus if thou try thy daily deeds, and pleasure in this pain,
Thy life shall cleanse thy corn from weeds, & shine shall be
ye gain:
But if thy sinful sluggish eye, will venture for to wink,
Before thy wading will may try, how far thy soul may sink,
Beware and wake, for else thy bed, which soft & smooth is
made
May heap more harm upon thy head, than blows of enemy's
blade.
Thus if this pain procure thine ease, in bed as thou dost lie,
Perhaps it shall not God displease, to sing thus soberly:
I see that sleep is lent me here, to ease my weary bones,
As death at last shall eke appear, to ease my grievous
groans.
My daily sports, my paunch full fed, have caused my drowsy
eye,
As careless life in quiet led, might cause my soul to die:
The stretching arms, the yawning breath, which I to bedward
use,

31

Are patterns of the pangs of death, when life will me refuse:
And of my bed each sundry part in shadows doth resemble
The sundry shapes of death, whose dart shall make my
                                        flesh to tremble.
My bed itself is like the grave, my sheets the winding sheet,
My clothes the molde which I must have, to cover me most
                                        meet:
The hungry fleas which frisk so fresh, to worms I can
                                        compare,
Which greedily shall gnaw my flesh, and leave the bones
                                        full bare:
The waking cock that early crows to wear the night away,
Puts in my mind the trump that blows before the latter day.
And as I rise up lustily, when sluggish sleep is past,
So hope I to rise joyfully, to Judgement at the last.
Thus will I wake, thus will I sleep, thus will I hope to rise,
Thus will I neither wail nor weep, but sing in godly wyse.
My bones shall in this bed remain, my soul in God shall
                                        trust,
By whom I hope to rise again from death and earthly dust.

And If I Did What Then?

And if I did what then?
Are you aggrieved therefore?
The sea hath fish for every man,
And what would you have more?

Thus did my mistress once
Amaze my mind with doubt:
And popt a question for the nonce
To beat my brains about.

Whereto I thus replied:
Each fisherman can wish
That all the sea at every tide
Were his alone to fish.

And so did I (in vain),
But since it may not be:
Let such fish there as find the gain,
And leave the loss for me.

And with such luck and loss
I will content my self:
Till tides of turning time may toss
Such fishers on the shelf.

And when they stick on sands,
That every man may see:
Then will I laugh and clap my hands,
As they do now at me.

The Feeble Thread

The feeble thread which *Lachesis* hath spun,
To draw my days in short abode with thee,
Hath wrought a web which now (well near) is done,
The wale is worn: and (all too late) I see
That lingering life doth dally but in vain,
For *Atropos* will cut the twist in twain.

I not discern what life but loathsome were,
When faithful friends are kept in twain by want:
Nor yet perceive what pleasure doth appear,
To deep desires where good success is scant.
Such spite yet shows dame fortune (if she frown),
The haughty hearts in high mishaps to drown.

Hot be the flames which boil in friendly minds,
Cruel the care and dreadful is the doom:
Slipper the knot which tract of time untwynds,
Hateful the life and welcome were the tomb.
Blessed were the day which might devour such youth,
And cursed the want that seeks to choke such truth.

This wailing verse I bathe in flowing tears,
And would my life might end with these my lines:
Yet strive I not to force into thine ears,
Such fained plaints as fickle faith resigns.
But high forsight in dreams hath stopped my breath,
And caused the Swan to sing before his death.

For lo these naked walls do well declare,
My latest leave of thee I taken have:
And unknown coasts which I must seek with care
Do well divine that there shall be my grave:
There shall my death make many for to moan,

Scarce known to them, well known to thee alone.

This boon of thee (as last request) I crave,
When true report shall sound my death with fame:
Vouchsafe yet then to go unto my grave,
And there first write my birth and then my name:
And how my life was shortened many years,
By women's wiles as to the world appears.

And in reward of grant to this request,
Permit O God my tongue these words to tell:
(When as his pen shall write upon my chest)
With shrieking voice mine own dear friend farewell.
No care on earth did seem so much to me,
As when my corpse was forced to part from thee.

Counsel given to master Bartholmew Withipoll
a little before his latter journey to Geane, 1572

Mine own good *Bat*, before thou hoist up sail,
To make a furrow in the foaming seas,
Content thyself to hear for thine avail,
Such harmless words, as ought thee not displease.
First in thy journey, jape not over much,
What? laughest thou *Batte*, because I write so plain?
Believe me now it is a friendly touch,
To use few words where friendship doth remain.
And for I find, that fault hath run too fast,
Both in thy flesh, and fancy too sometime,   10
Me thinks plain dealing biddeth me to cast
This bone at first amid my doggerel rhyme.
But shall I say, to give thee grave advice?
(Which in my head is [God he knowes] full geazon)?
Then mark me well, and though I be not wise,
Yet in my rhyme, thou mayest perhaps find reason.
First every day, beseech thy God on knee,
So to direct thy staggering steps alway,
That he which every secret thought doth see
May hold thee in, when thou wouldst go astray: 20
And that he deign to send thee safe retoure,
And quick dispatch of that which is thy due:
Let this my *Batte* be both thy prime and hour,
Wherin also commend to *Nostre Dieu*,
Thy good Companion and my very friend,
To whom I should (but time would not permit)
Have taken pain some ragged rhyme to send
In trusty token, that I not forget
His courtesy: but this is debt to thee,
I promised it, and now I mean to pay: 30
What was I saying? Sirra, will you see
How soon my wits were wandering astray?

36

I say, pray thou for thee and for thy mate,
So shipmen sing, and though the note be plain,
Yet sure the music is in heavenly state,
When friends sing so, and know not how to feign.
Then next to G O D, thy Prince have still in mind
Thy country's honour, and the common wealth:
And flee from them, which fled with every wind
From native soil, to foreign coasts by stealth: 40
Their trains are trustless, tending still to treason,
Their smoothed tongues are lined all with guile,
Their power slender, scarcely worth two peason,
Their malice much, their wits are full of wile:
Eschew them then, and when thou seest them, say,
Da, da, sir *K,* I may not come at you,
You cast a snare your country to betray,
And would you have me trust you now for true?
Remember *Batte* the foolish blink-eyed boy
Which was at Rome, thou knowest whom I mean,   50
Remember eke the pretty beardless toy,
Whereby thou foundst a safe return to *Geane,*
Do so again: (God shield thou shouldst have need),
But rather so, than to forswear thy self:
A loyal heart, (believe this as thy Creed)
Is evermore more worth than worldly pelf.
And for one lesson, take this more of me,
There are three Ps almost in every place,
From which I counsel thee always to flee,
And take good heed of them in any case,   60
The first is poison, perilous indeed
To such as travel with a heavy purse:
And thou my *Batte* beware, for thou hast need,
Thy purse is lined with paper, which is worse:
Thy bills of credit will not they thinkst thou,
Be bait to sette *Italian* hands on work?
Yes by my faye, and never worse than now,

When every knave hath leisure for to lurk,
And knoweth thou comest for the shells of Christ:
Beware therefore, wherever that thou go, 70
It may fall out that thou shalt be enticed
To sup sometimes with a *Magnifico*,
And have a *fico* foisted in thy dish,
Because thou shouldst digest thy meat the better:
Beware therefore, and rather feed on fish,
Than learn to spell fine flesh with such a Letter.
Some may present thee with a pound or twain
Of Spanish soap to wash thy linen white:
Beware therefore, and think it were small gain,
To save thy shirt, and cast thy skin off quite: 80
Some cunning man may teach thee for to ride,
And stuff thy saddle all with Spanish wool,
Or in thy stirrups have a toy so tied,
As both thy legs may swell thy buskins full:
Beware therefore, and bear a noble port,
Drink not for thirst before another taste:
Let none outlandish tailor take disporte
To stuff thy doublet full of such Bumbaste,
As it may cast thee in unkindly sweat,
And cause thy hair per company to glide, 90
Strangers are fine in many a proper feat:
Beware therefore: the second *P.* is Pride,
More perilous than was the first by far,
For that infects but blood and leaves the bones,
This poisons all, and minds of men doth mar,
It findeth nooks to creep in for the nones:
First from the mind it makes the heart to swell,
From thence the flesh is pampered every part,
The skin is taught in dyer's shops to dwell,
The hair is curled or frizzled up by art: 100
Believe me *Batte*, our countrymen of late
Have caught such knacks abroad in foreign land,

That most men call them *Devils incarnate*,
So singular in their conceits they stand:
Now sir, if I shall see your mastership
Come home disguised and clad in quaint array,
As with a piketooth biting on your lip,
Your brave *Mustachyos* turned the *Turky* way,
A Coptanckt hat made on a Flemish block,
A nightgown cloak down trailing to your toes,   110
A slender sloppe close couched to your docke,
A curtold slipper, and a short silk hose:
Bearing your rapier point above the hilt,
And looking big like *Marquise of all Beef*,
Then shall I count your toil and travel spilt,
Because my second *P*, with you is chief.
But forwards now, although I stayed a while,
My hindmost *P*, is worse than both these two,
For it both bones and body doth defile,
With fouler blots than both those other do.   120
Short tale to make, this *P*, can bear no blocks,
(God shield me *Batte*, should bear it in his breast)
And with a dash it spelleth piles and pocks
A parlous *P*, and worse than both the rest:
Now though I find no cause for to suspect
My *Batte* in this, because he hath been tried,
Yet since such Spanish buttons can infect
Kings, Emperors, Princes and the world so wide,
And since those suns do mellow men so fast
As most that travel come home very ripe
Although (by sweat) they learn to live and last   130
When they have danced after Guido's pipe:
Therefore I thought it meet to warn my friend
Of this foul *P*, and so an end of *P*s.
Now for thy diet mark my tale to end,
And thank me then, for that is all my fees.
See thou exceed not in three double U's,

The first is Wine, which may inflame thy blood,
The second, Women, such as haunt the stews,
The third is Wilfulness, which doth no good.   140
These three eschew, or temper them always:
So shall my *Batte* prolong his youthful years,
And see long *George* again, with happy days,
Who if he be as faithful to his fears,
As he was wont, will daily pray for *Batte*,
And for *Pencoyde*: and if it fall out so,
That *James a Parrye* do but make good that,
Which he hath said: and if he be (no, no)
The best companion that long *George* can find,
Then at the Spa I promise for to be   150
In *August* next, if God turn not my mind,
Where as I would be glad thyself to see:
Till then farewell, and thus I end my song,
Take it in gree, for else thou doest me wrong.

The Lullaby of a Lover

Sing lullaby, as women do,
Wherewith they bring their babes to rest,
And lullaby can I sing too,
As womanly as can the best.
With lullaby they still the child,
And if I be not much beguiled,
Full many wanton babes have I
Which must be stilled with lullaby.

First lullaby my youthful years,
It is now time to go to bed,
For crooked age and hoary hairs,
Have won the haven within my head:
With Lullaby then youth be still,
With Lullaby content thy will,
Since courage quails, and comes behind,
Go sleep, and so beguile thy mind.

Next Lullaby my gazing eyes,
Which wonted were to glance apace.
For every glass may now suffice,
To show the furrows in my face:
With Lullaby then wink awhile,
With Lullaby your looks beguile:
Let no fair face, nor beauty bright
Entice you efte with vain delight.

And Lullaby my wanton will,
Let reason's rule now reign thy thought,
Since all too late I find by skill,
How dear I have thy fancies bought:
With Lullaby now take thine ease,
With Lullaby thy doubts appease:

41

For trust to this, if thou be still,
My body shall obey thy will.

Eke Lullaby my loving boy,
My little Robin take thy rest,
Since age is cold, and nothing coy,
Keep close thy coyne, for so is best:
With Lullaby be thou content,
With Lullaby thy lusts relent,
Let others pay which hath mo pence,
Thou art too poor for such expense.

Thus Lullaby my youth, mine eyes,
My will, my ware, and all that was,
I can no mo delays devise,
But welcome pain, let pleasure pass:
With Lullaby now take your leave,
With Lullaby your dreams deceive,
And when you rise with waking eye,
Remember then this Lullaby.

Despised Things May Live

Despised things may live, although they pine in pain:
And things oft trodden underfoot, may once yet rise again.
The stone that lieth full low, may climb at last full high:
And stand aloft on stately towers, in sight of every eye.
The cruel axe which fells the tree that grew full straight: 5
Is worn with rust, when it renews, and springeth up on
                                height.
The roots of rotten reeds in swelling seas are seen:
And when each tide hath tossed his worst, they grow again
                            full green.
Thus much to please myself, unpleasantly I sing.   9
And shrich to ease my morning mind, in spite of envies
                                sting.
I am now set full light, who erst was dearly loved:
Some newfound choice is more esteemed, than that which
                          well was proved.
Some Diomede is crept into Dame Cressida's heart:
And trusty Troilus now is taught in vain to playne his part.
What resteth then for me? but thus to wade in woe: 15
And hang in hope of better chance, when change appointeth
                                so.
I see no sight on earth, but it to change inclines:
As little clouds oft overcast, the brightest sun that shines.
No flower is so fresh, but frost can it deface:
No man so sure in any seat, but he may leese his place.   20
So that I stand content (though much against my mind)
To take in worth this loathsome lot, which luck to me
                            assigned,
And trust to see the time, when they that now are up:
May feel the whirl of fortune's wheel, and test of sorrow's
                                cup.
God knoweth I wish it not, it had been bet for me: 25
Still to have kept my quiet chayre in hap of high degree.

But since without recure, Dame Change in love must reign:
I now wish change that sought no change, but constant did
remain.
And if such change do chance, I vow to clap my hands,
And laugh at them which laughed at me: lo thus my fancy
stands.

In Broken Sleeps

When steadfast friendship (bound by holy oath)
Did part perforce my presence from thy sight
In dreams I might behold how thou wert loth
With troubled thoughts to part from thy delight.
When Poplar walls enclosed thy pensive mind,
My painted shadow did thy woes receive:
Thine evening walks by Thames in open wind,
Did long to see my sailing boat arrive.
But when the dismold day did seek to part
From London walls thy longing mind for me,
The sugared kisses (sent to thy dear heart)
With secret smart in broken sleeps I see.
Wherefore in tears I drench a thousand fold,
Till these moist eyes thy beauty may behold.

Magnum vectigal parcimonia

The common speech is, spend and God will send,
But what sends he? a bottle and a bag,
A staff, a wallet and a woeful end,
For such as list in bravery so to brag.
Then if thou covet coin enough to spend,
Learn first to spare thy budget at the brink,
So shall the bottom be the faster bound:
But he that list with lavish hand to link,
(In like expense) a penny with a pound,
May chance at last to sit aside and shrink   10
His harebrained head without dame dainty's door.
Hick, Hobbe, and Dick, with clouts upon their knee,
Have many times more goonhole groats in store
And change of crowns more quick at call then he,
Which let their lease and took their rent before.
For he that raps a royal on his cap,
Before he put one penny in his purse,
Had need turn quick and broach a better tap,
Or else his drink may chance go down the worse.
I not deny but some men have good hap,   20
To climb aloft by scales of courtly grace,
And win the world with liberality:
Yet he that yerks old angels out apace,
And hath no new to purchase dignity,
When orders fall, may chance to lack his grace.
For haggard hawks mislike an empty hand:
So stiffly some stick to the mercer's stall,
Till suits of silk have sweat out all their land.
So oft thy neighbours banquet in thy hall,
Till Davie Debet in thy parlour stand,   30
And bids thee welcome to thine own decay.
I like a lion's looks not worth a leek
When every fox beguiles him of his prey:

45

What sauce but sorrow serveth him a week,
Which all his cates consumeth in one day?
First use thy stomach to a stand of ale,
Before thy Malmesey come in merchants' books,
And rather wear (for shift) thy shirt of mail,
Than tear thy silken sleeves with tenter hooks,
Put feathers in thy pillows great and small,   40
Let them be princkt with plumes, that gape for plums,
Heap up both gold and silver safe in hooches,
Catch, snatch, and scratch for scrapings and for crumbs
Before thou deck thy hat (on high) with brooches.
Let first thine one hand hold fast all that comes,
Before that other learn his letting fly:
Remember still that soft fire makes sweet malt,
No haste but good (who means to multiply):
Bought wit is dear, and dressed with sour salt,
Repentance comes too late, and then say I,
Who spares the first and keeps the last unspent,
Shall find that sparing yields a goodly rent.

Sic tuli.

Gascoigne's Woodmanship

My worthy Lord, I pray you wonder not,
To see your woodman shoot so oft awry,
Nor that he stands amazed like a sot,
And lets the harmless deer (unhurt) go by.
Or if he strike a doe which is but carren,
Laugh not good Lord, but favour such a fault,
Take well in worth, he would fain hit the barren,
But though his heart be good, his hap is naught:
And therefore now I crave your Lordship's leave,
To tell you plain what is the cause of this: 10
First if it please your honour to perceive,
What makes your woodman shoot so oft amiss,
Believe me Lord the case is nothing strange,
He shoots awry almost at every mark,
His eyes have been so used for to range,
That now God knows they be both dim and dark.
For proof he bears the note of folly now,
Who shot sometimes to hit Philosophy,
And ask you why? forsooth I make avow,
Because his wanton wits went all awry.   20
Next that, he shot to be a man of law,
And spent some time with learned Littleton,
Yet in the end, he proved but a daw,
For law was dark and he had quickly done.
Then could he wish Fitzherbert such a brain,
As Tully had, to write the law by art,
So that with pleasure, or with little pain,
He might perhaps, have caught a truant's part.
But all too late, he most misliked the thing,
Which most might help to guide his arrow straight: 30
He winked wrong, and so let slip the string,
Which cast him wide, for all his quaint conceit.
From thence he shot to catch a courtly grace,

47

And thought even there to wield the world at will,
But out alas he much mistook the place,
And shot awry at every rover still.
The blazing baits which draw the gazing eye,
Unfeathered there his first affection,
No wonder then although he shot awry,
Wanting the feathers of discretion.   40
Yet more than them, the marks of dignity,
He much mistook and shot the wronger way,
Thinking the purse of prodigality,
Had been best mean to purchase such a prey.
He thought the flattering face which fleareth still,
Had been full fraught with all fidelity,
And that such words as courtiers use at will,
Could not have varied from the verity.
But when his bonnet buttoned with gold,
His comely cape begarded all with gay,   50
His bumbast hose, with linings manifold,
His knit silk stocks and all his quaint array,
Had picked his purse of all the Peter pence,
Which might have paid for his promotion,
Then (all too late) he found that light expense,
Had quite quenched out the court's devotion.
So that since then the taste of misery,
Hath been always full bitter in his bit,
And why? forsooth because he shot awry,
Mistaking still the marks which others hit.   60
But now behold what mark the man doth find,
He shoots to be a soldier in his age,
Mistrusting all the virtues of the mind,
He trusts the power of his personage.
As though long limbs led by a lusty heart,
Might yet suffice to make him rich again,
But Flushing frays have taught him such a part,
That now he thinks the wars yield no such gain.

And sure I fear, unless your lordship deign,
To train him yet into some better trade, 70
It will be long before he hit the vein,
Whereby he may a richer man be made.
He cannot climb as other catchers can
To lead a charge before himself be led,
He cannot spoil the simple sakeless man,
Which is content to feed him with his bread.
He cannot pinch the painful soldier's pay,
And shear him out his share in ragged sheets,
He cannot stop to take a greedy prey
Upon his fellows groveling in the streets. 80
He cannot pull the spoil from such as pill,
And seem full angry at such foul offence,
Although the gain content his greedy will,
Under the cloak of contrary pretence:
And nowadays, the man that shoots not so,
May shoot amiss, even as your woodman doth:
But then you marvel why I let them go,
And never shoot, but say farewell forsooth:
Alas my Lord, while I do muse hereon,
And call to mind my youthful years misspent, 90
They give me such a bone to gnaw upon,
That all my senses are in silence pent.
My mind is rapt in contemplation,
Wherein my dazzled eyes only behold,
The black hour of my constellation,
Which framed me so luckless on the molde:
Yet therewithall I cannot but confess,
That vain presumption makes my heart to swell,
For thus I think, not all the world (I guess),
Shoots better than I, nay some shoot not so well. 100
In Aristotle somewhat did I learn,
To guide my manners all by comeliness,
And Tully taught me somewhat to discern

Between sweet speech and barbarous rudeness.
Old Parkins, Rastall, and Dan Bracten's books,
Did lend me somewhat of the lawless Law,
The crafty courtiers with their guileful looks,
Must needs put some experience in my maw:
Yet cannot these with many masteries mo,
Make me shoot straight at any gainful prick,   110
Where some that never handled such a bow,
Can hit the white, or touch it near the quick,
Who can nor speak, nor write in pleasant wise,
Nor lead their life by Aristotle's rule,
Nor argue well on questions that arise,
Nor plead a case more than my Lord Mayor's mule,
Yet can they hit the marks that I do miss,
And win the mean which may the man maintain.
Now when my mind doth mumble upon this,
No wonder then although I pine for pain: 120
And whiles mine eyes behold this mirror thus,
The herd goeth by, and farewell gentle does:
So that your Lordship quickly may discuss
What blinds mine eyes so oft (as I suppose).
But since my Muse can to my Lord rehearse
What makes me miss, and why I do not shoot,
Let me imagine in this worthless verse,
If right before me, at my standings foot
There stood a doe, and I should strike her dead,
And then she prove a carrion carcase too,   130
What figure might I find within my head,
To 'scuse the rage which ruled me so to do?
Some might interpret by plain paraphrase,
That lack of skill or fortune led the chance,
But I must otherwise expound the case,
I say Jehova did this doe advance,
And made her bold to stand before me so,
Till I had thrust mine arrow to her heart,

That by the sodaine of her overthrow,
I might endeavour to amend my part,   140
And turn mine eyes that they no more behold,
Such guileful marks as seem more than they be:
And though they glister outwardly like gold,
Are inwardly but brass, as men may see:
And when I see the milk hang in her teat,
Methinks it sayth, old babe now learn to suck,
Who in thy youth couldst never learn the feat
To hit the whites which live with all good luck.
Thus have I told my Lord, (God grant in season)
A tedious tale in rhyme, but little reason.   150

The Lover

I groped in thy pocket pretty peat,
And found a lemon which I looked not:
So found I once (which now I must repeat)
Both leaves and letters which I liked not.
Such hap have I to find and seek it not,
But since I see no faster means to bind them,
I will (henceforth) take lemmans as I find them.

The Woman's Reply

A lemon (but no lemman) Sir you found,
For lemmans bear their name too broad before:
The which since it hath given you such a wound,
That you seem now offended very sore:
Content yourself you shall find (there) no more.
But take your lemmans henceforth where you lust,
For I will show my letters where I trust.

Gascoigne's Voyage into Holland in 1572

A strange conceit, a vein of new delight,
Twixt weale and woe, twixt joy and bitter grief,
Hath pricked forth my hasty pen to write
This worthless verse in hazard of reproof:
And to mine *Alderlievest* Lord I must endite
A woeful case, a chip of sorry chance,
A type of heaven, a lively hue of hell,
A fear to fall, a hope of high advance,
A life, a death, a dreary tale to tell
But since I know the pith of my pastaunce   10
Shall most consist in telling of a truth,
Vouchsafe my Lord (*en bon gré*) for to take
This trusty tale the story of my youth,
This Chronicle which of myself I make,
To show my Lord what helpless hap ensueth,
When heady youth will gad without a guide,
And range untied in lease of liberty,
Or when bare need a starting hole hath spied
To peep abroad from mother Misery,
And buildeth castles in the welkin wide,   20
In hope thereby to dwell with wealth and ease.
But he the Lord (whom my good Lord doth know)
Can bind or lose, as best to him shall please,
Can save or spill, raise up or overthrow,
Can gauld with grief, and yet the pain appease.
Which thing to prove if so my Lord take time,
(When greater cares his head shall not possess)
To sit and read this ranging ragged rhyme,
I doubt not then but that he will confess
What falls I found when last I leapt to climb.   30
In March it was, that cannot I forget,
In this last March upon the ninetenth day,
When from Gravesend in boat I gan to jette

To board our ship in Quinborough that lay,
From whence the very twentieth day we set
Our sails abroad to slice the salt sea foam,
And anchors weighed gan trust the trustless flood:
That day and night amid the waves we roam
To seek the coast of Holland where it stood.
And on the next when we were far from home,   40
And near the haven whereto we sought to sail,
A ferly chaunce: (whereon alone to think
My hand now quakes, and all my senses fail)
Gan us befall: the pilot gan to shrink,
And all aghast his courage seemed to quail.
Whereat amazed, the Master and his mate
Gan ask the cause of his so sudden change,
And from aloft the Steward of our state,
(The sounding plumb) in haste post-haste must range,
To try the depth and goodness of our gate.   50
Methinks (even yet) I hear his heavy voice
Fathom three, four, foot more, foot less, that cried:
Methinks I hear the fearful whispering noise,
Of such as said full softly (me beside)
God grant this journey cause us to rejoice
When I poor soul, which close in cabin lay,
And there had retched till gall was well near burst,
With giddy head, my stumbling steps must stay
To look abroad as boldly as I durst.
And whiles I hearken what the sailors say,   60
The sounder sings, fathom two full no more.
Aloof, aloof, then cried the Master out,
The Steersmate strives to send us from the shore,
And trusts the stream, whereof we erst had doubt,
Tween two extremes thus were we tossed sore,
And went to Hull, until we leisure had
To talk at large, and eke to know the cause
What mood had made our pilot look so sad.

At last the Dutch with butterbitten jaws,
(For so he was a Dutch, a devil, a swadde,   70
A fool, a drunkard, or a traitor tone)
Gan answer thus: *Ghy zijt te vroegh* here come,
Tis niet goet tijt and standing all alone,
Gan preach to us, which fools were all and some
To trust him fool, in whom there skill was none.
Or what knew we if Alba's subtle brain
(So to prevent our enterprise by treason)
Had him suborned to tice us to this train
And so himself (per company and season)
For spite, for hate, or else for hope of gain.   80
This must we think that Alba would not spare
To give out gold for such a sinful deed:
And glistering gold can oftentimes ensnare,
More perfect wits than Holland soil doth breed.
But let that pass, and let us now compare
Our own fond fact with this his foul offence.
We knew him not, nor where he wond that time,
Nor if he had pilot's experience,
Or pilot's craft, to clear himself from crime.
Yea more than that (how void were we of sense)   90
We had small smacke of any tale he told,
He poured out Dutch to drown us all in drink,
And we (wise men) upon his words were bold,
To run on head: but let me now bethink
The master's speech: and let me so unfold
The depth of all this foolish oversight.
The Master spoke even like a skilful man,
And said I sail the seas both day and night,
I know the tides as well as other can,
From pole to pole I can the courses plight: 100
I know France, Spain, Greece, Denmark, Daunsk & all,
Frize, Flanders, Holland, every coast I know,
But truth to tell, it seldom doth befall,

That English merchants ever bend their bow
To shoot at Breyll, where now our flight should fall,
They send their shafts farther for greater gain.
So that this haven is yet (quoth he) uncouth,
And God grant now that England may attain
Such gains by Breyll, (a gospel on that mouth)
As is desired: thus spoke the Master plain.   110
And since (said he) myself knew not the sowne,
How could I well a better pilot find,
Than this (which first) did say he dwelt in town,
And knew the way wherever sat the wind?
While we thus talk, all sails are taken down,
And we to Hull (as erst I said) gan wend,
Till full two hours and somewhat more were past.
Our guide then spoke in Dutch and bade us bend
All sails again: for now quod he (at last)
Die tijt is goet, dat heb ick weell bekend.   120
Why stay I long to end a woeful tale?
We trust his Dutch, and up the foresail goes,
We fall on knees amid the happy gale,
(Which by God's will full kind and calmly blows)
And unto him we there unfold our bale,
Whereon to think I write and weep for joy,
That pleasant song the hundred and seventh Psalm,
There did we read to comfort our annoy,
Which to my soul (methought) was sweet as balm,
Yea far more sweet than any worldly toy.   130
And when he had with prayers praised the Lord,
Our *Edell Bloetts*, gan fall to eat and drink,
And for their sauce, at taking up the board
The ship so struck (as all we thought to sink)
Against the ground. Then all with one accord
We fell again on knees to pray apace,
And therewithall even at the second blow,
(The number cannot from my mind outpace)

55

Our helm struck of, and we must fleet and flow,
Where wind and waves would guide us by their grace.   140
The wind waxed calm as I have said before,
(O mighty God so didst thou swage our woes)
The selly ship was sowst and smitten sore,
With counter buffets, blows and double blows.
At last the keel which might endure no more,
Gan rend in twain and sucks the water in:
Then might you see pale looks and woeful cheer,
Then might you hear loud cries and deadly din:
Well noble minds in perils best appear,
And boldest hearts in bale will never blinne.   150
For there were some (of whom I will not say
That I was one) which never changed hue,
But pumped apace, and laboured every way
To save themselves, and all their lovely crew,
Which cast the best freight overboard away,
Both corn and cloth, and all that was of weight,
Which hauled and pulled at every helping cord,
Which prayed to God and made their conscience straight.
As for myself: I here protest my Lord,
My words were these: O God in heaven on height,   160
Behold me not as now a wicked wight,
A sack of sin, a wretch enwrapped in wrath,
Let no fault past (O Lord) offend thy sight,
But weigh my will which now those faults doth loathe,
And of thy mercy pity this our plight.
Even thou good God which of thy grace didst say
That for one good, thou wouldst all Sodom save,
Behold us all: thy shining beams display,
Some here (I trust) thy goodness shall engrave,
To be chaste vessels unto Thee always,   170
And so to live in honour of Thy name:
Believe me Lord, thus to the Lord I said.
But there were some (alas the more their blame)

56

Which in the pump their only comfort laid,
And trusted that to turn our grief to game.
Alas (quod I) our pump good God must be,
Our sail, our stern, our tackling, and our trust.
Some other cried to clear the shipboat free,
To save the chief and leave the rest in dust.
Which word once spoke (a wondrous thing to see)   180
All haste post-haste, was made to have it done:
And up it comes in haste much more than speed.
There did I see a woeful work begun,
Which now (even now) doth make my heart to bleed.
Some made such haste that in the boat they won,
Before it was above the hatches brought.
Strange tale to tell, what haste some men shall make
To find their death before the same be sought.
Some twixt the boat and ship their bane do take,
Both drowned and slain with brains for haste crushed out.
At last the boat half freighted in the air   191
Is hoist aloft, and on the seas down set,
When I that yet in God could not despair,
Still plied the pump, and patiently did let
All such take boat as thither made repair.
And herewithall I safely may protest
I might have won the boat as well as one,
And had that seemed a safety for the rest
I should percase even with the first have gone.
But when I saw the boat was over pressed   200
And pestred full with more than it might bear,
And therewithall with cheerful look might see
My chief companions whom I held most dear
(Whose company had thither trained me)
Abiding still aboard our ship yfeare:
Nay then (quoth I) good God thy will be done,
For with my fears I will both live and die.
And ere the boat far from our sight was gone

The wave so wrought, that they (which thought to flee
And so to scape) with waves were over-run.   210
Lo how he strives in vain that strives with God
For there we lost the flower of the band,
And of our crew full twenty souls and odd,
The sea sucks up, whiles we on hatches stand
In smarting fear to feel that selfsame rod.
Well on (as yet) our battered bark did pass,
And brought the rest within a mile of land,
Then thought I sure now need not I to pass,
For I can swim and so escape this sand.
Thus did I deem all careless like an ass,   220
When suddenly the wind our foresail took,
And turned about and brought us eft to seas.
Then cried we all cast out the anchor hook,
And here let bide, such help as God may please:
Which anchor cast, we soon the same forsook,
And cut it off, for fear lest thereupon
Our ship should bowge, then called we fast for fire,
And so discharged our great guns everyone,
To warn the town thereby of our desire:
But all in vain, for succour sent they none.   230
At last a hoy from sea came flinging fast,
And towards us held course as straight as line.
Then might you see our hands to heaven up cast
To render thanks unto the power divine,
That so vouchsafed to save us yet at last:
But when this hoy gan (well near) board our bark,
And might perceive what peril we were in,
It turned away and left us still in carke,
This tale is true (for now to lie were sin)
It left us there in dread and dangers dark.   240
It left us so, and that within the sight
And hearing both of all the pier at Breyll.
Now ply thee pen, and paint the foul despite

58

Of drunken Dutchmen standing there even still,
For whom we came in their cause for to fight,
For whom we came their state for to defend,
For whom we came as friends to grieve their foes,
They now disdained (in this distress) to lend
One helping boat for to assuage our woes:
They saw our harms the which they would not mend,   250
And had not been that God even then did raise
Some instruments to succour us at need,
We had been sunk and swallowed all in seas.
But God's will was (in way of our good speed)
That on the pier (lamenting our mysease)
Some English were, whose naked swords did force
The drunken Dutch, the cankered churls to come,
And so at last (not moved by remorse,
But forced by fear) they sent us succour some:
Some must I say: and for to tell the course,   260
They sent us succour sauced with sour despite,
They saved our lives and spoiled us of the rest,
They stole our goods by day and eke by night,
They showed the worst and closely kept the best.
And in this time (this treason must I write)
Our pilot fled, but how? not empty handed:
He fled from us, and with him did convey
A hoy full fraught (whiles we meanwhile were landed)
With powder, shot, and all our best array:
This skill he had, for all he set us sanded.   270
And now my Lord, declare your noble mind,
Was this a pilot, or a Pilate judge?
Or rather was he not of Judas kind:
Which left us thus and close away could trudge?
Well, at the Bryell to tell you what we find,
The Governor was all bedewed with drink,
His trulls and he were all laid down to sleep,
And we must shift, and of ourselves must think

What mean was best, and how we best might keep
That yet remained: the rest was close in clink.   280
Well, on our knees with trickling tears of joy,
We gave God thanks: and as we might, did learn
What might be found in every pynke and hoy.
And thus my Lord, your honour may discern
Our perils past, and how in our annoy
God saved me (your Lordship's bound for ever)
Who else should not be able now to tell,
The state wherein this country doth persevere,
Nor how they seem in careless minds to dwell.
(So did they erst and so they will do ever)   290
And to my Lord for to bewray my mind
Me thinks they be a race of Bulbeef born,
Whose hearts their butter mollyfyeth by kind,
And so the force of beef is clean outworn:
And eke their brains with double beer are lined:
So that they march bumbast with buttered beer,
Like sops of browesse puffed up with froth,
Where inwardly they be but hollow gear,
As weak as wind, which with one puff up goeth:
And yet they brag, and think they have no peer,   300
Because Haarlem hath hitherto held out,
Although indeed (as they have suffered Spain)
The end thereof even now doth rest in doubt.
Well, as for that, let it (for me) remain
In God his hands, whose hand hath brought me out,
To tell my Lord this tale now tane in hand,
As how they train their treasons all in drink,
And when themselves for drink can scarcely stand,
Yet suck out secrets (as themselves do think)
From guests. The best (almost) in all their land,   310
(I name no man, for that were brode before)
Will (as men say) enure the same sometime,
But surely this (or I mistake him sore)

60

Or else he can (but let it pass in rhyme)
Dissemble deep, and mock sometimes the more:
Well, drunkenness is here good company,
And therewithall *per consequence* it falls
That whoredom is accounted jollity:
A gentle state, where two such tennis balls
Are tossed still and better bowls let lie.   320
I cannot herewith from my Lord conceal,
How God and Mammon here do dwell yfeare,
And how the Mass is cloaked under veil
Of policy, till all the coast be clear.
Ne can I choose, but I must ring a peal,
To tell what hypocrites the nuns here be:
And how the old nuns be content to go,
Before a man in streets like mother B,
Until they come wheras there dwells a Ho,
(Receive that half, and let the rest go free)   330
There can they point with finger as they pass,
Yea sir, sometimes they can come in themself,
To strike the bargain tween a wanton lass,
And *Edel bloets*: now is not this good pelf?
As for the young nuns, they be bright as glass,
And chaste forsooth, *met v*: and *anders niet*:
What said I? what? that is a mystery,
I may no verse of such a theme indict,
Young Rowland Yorke may tell it bet than I
Yet to my Lord this little will I write,   340
That though I have (myself) no skill at all,
To take the countenance of a Colonel,
Had I a good Lieutenant general,
As good John Zuche wherever that he dwell,
Or else Ned Dennye (fair mought him befall)
I could have brought a noble regiment
Of smugskinned nuns into my country soil:
But farewell they as things impertinent,

Let them (for me) go dwell with master Moyle,
Who hath behight to place them well in Kent.   350
And I shall well my selly self content,
To come alone unto my lovely Lord,
And unto him (when rhyming sport is spent)
To tell some sad and reasonable word,
Of Holland's state, the which I will present,
In charts, in maps, and eke in models made,
If God of heaven my purpose not prevent.
And in meanwhile although my wits do wade
In ranging rhyme, and fling some folly forth,
I trust my Lord will take it well in worth.   360

The Green Knight's Farewell to Fancy

Fancy (quoth he) farewell, whose badge I long did bear,
And in my hat full harebrainedly, thy flowers did I wear:
Too late I find (at last), thy fruits are nothing worth,
Thy blossoms fall & fade full fast, though bravery bring
                                                    them forth.
By thee I hoped always, in deep delights to dwell,
But since I find thy fickleness, *Fancy* (quoth he) *farewell*.

Thou madst me live in love, which wisdom bids me hate,
Thou bleardst mine eyes & madst me think, that faith was
                                                    mine by fate:
By thee those bitter sweets, did please my taste alway,
By thee I thought that love was light, and pain was but a
                                                    play:

I thought that Beauty's blaze, was meet to bear the bell,
And since I find myself deceived, *Fancy* (quoth he) *farewell*.

The gloss of gorgeous courts, by thee did please mine eye,
A stately sight me thought it was, to see the brave go by:
To see their feathers flaunt, to mark their strange devise,
To lie along in ladies' laps, to lisp and make it nice:
To fawn and flatter both, I liked sometimes well,
But since I see how vain it is, *Fancy* (quoth he) *farewell*.

When court had cast me off, I toiled at the plough   19
My fancy stood in strange conceits, to thrive I wot not how:
By mills, by making malt, by sheep and eke by swine,
By duck and drake, by pig and goose, by calves & keeping
                                                          kine:
By feeding bullocks fat, when price at markets fell,
But since my swains eat up my gains, *Fancy* (quoth he)
                                                     farewell.

In hunting of the deer, my fancy took delight,
All forests knew, my folly still, the moonshine was my light:
In frosts I felt no cold, a sunburnt hue was best,
I sweat and was in temper still, my watching seemed rest:
What dangers deep I passed, it folly were to tell,   29
And since I sigh to think thereon, *Fancy* (quoth he) *farewell*.

A fancy fed me once, to write in verse and rhyme,
To wray my grief, to crave reward, to cover still my crime:
To frame a long discourse, on stirring of a straw,
To rumble rhyme in raff and ruff, yet all not worth an haw:
To hear it said there goeth, the *Man that writes so well*,
But since I see, what poets be, *Fancy* (quoth he) *farewell*.

At music's sacred sound, my fancies eft begun,
In concords, discords, notes and clefs, in tunes of unison:

In hierarchies and strains, in rests, in rule and space,   39
In monochords and moving moods, in burdens under base:
In descants and in chants, I strained many a yell,
But since musicians be so mad, *Fancy* (quoth he) *farewell*.

To plant strange country fruits, to sow such seeds likewise,
To dig & delve for new found roots, where old might well
                                                        suffice:
To prune the water boughs, to pick the mossy trees,
(Oh how it pleased my fancy once) to kneel upon my knees,
To griffe a pippin stock, when sap begins to swell: 47
But since the gains scarce quite the cost, *Fancy* (quoth he)
                                                     farewell.

Fancy (quoth he) *farewell*, which made me follow drums
Where powdered bullets serves for sauce, to every dish that
                                                        comes:
Where treason lurks in trust, where hope all hearts beguiles,
Where mischief lieth still in wait, when fortune friendly
                                                        smiles:
Where one day's prison proves, that all such heavens are
                                                        hell,
And such I feel the fruits thereof, *Fancy* (quoth he) *farewell*.

If reason rule my thoughts, and God vouchsafe me grace
Then comfort of philosophy, shall make me change my race:
And fond I shall it find, that Fancy sets to show,
For weakly stands that building still, which lacketh grace
                                                        below:
But since I must accept, my fortunes as they fell,   59
I say God send me better speed, and *Fancy now farewell*.

Gascoigne's De Profundis

From depth of dole wherein my soul doth dwell,
From heavy heart which harbours in my breast,
From troubled sprite which seldom taketh rest.
From hope of heaven, from dread of darksome hell.
O gracious God, to thee I cry and yell.
My God, my Lord, my lovely Lord alone,
To thee I call, to thee I make my moan.
And thou (good God) vouchsafe in gree to take,
This woefull plaint,
Wherein I faint.
Oh hear me then for thy great mercy's sake.

Oh bend thine ears attentively to hear,
Oh turn thine eyes, behold me how I wail,
O hearken Lord, give ear for mine avail,
O mark in mind the burdens that I bear:
See how I sink in sorrows everywhere.
Behold and see what dolours I endure,
Give ear and mark what plaints I put in ure.
Bend willing ear: and pity therewithall,
My wailing voice,
Which hath no choice.
But evermore upon thy name to call.

If thou good Lord shouldest take thy rod in hand,
If thou regard what sins are daily done,
If thou take hold where we our works begone,
If thou decree in Judgement for to stand,
And be extreme to see our 'scuses scanned,
If thou take note of everything amiss,
And write in rolls how frail our nature is,
O glorious God, O King, O Prince of power,
What mortal wight,

65

May then have light,
To feel thy frown, if thou have list to lour?

But thou art good, and hast of mercy store,
Thou not delights't to see a sinner fall,
Thou hearknest first, before we come to call.
Thine ears are set wide open evermore,
Before we knock thou comest to the door.
Thou art more pressed to hear a sinner cry,
Then he is quick to climb to thee on high.
Thy mighty name be praised then alway,
Let faith and fear,
True witness bear.
How fast they stand which on thy mercy stay.

I look for thee (my lovely Lord) therefore.
For thee I wait for thee I tarry still,
Mine eyes do long to gaze on thee my fill.
For thee I watch, for thee I pry and pore.
My Soul for thee attendeth evermore.
My Soul doth thirst to take of thee a taste,
My Soul desires with thee for to be placed.
And to thy word (which can no man deceive)
Mine only trust,
My love and lust
In confidence continually shall cleave.

Before the break or dawning of the day,
Before the light be seen in lofty skies,
Before the sun appear in pleasant wyse,
Before the watch (before the watch I say)
Before the ward that waits therefore alway:
My soul, my sense, my secret thought, my sprite,
My will, my wish, my joy, and my delight:
Unto the Lord that sits in heaven on high,

With hasty wing,
From me doth fling,
And striveth still, unto the Lord to fly.

O Israel, O household of the Lord,
O Abraham's brats, O brood of blessed seed,
O chosen sheep that love the Lord indeed:
O hungry hearts, feed still upon his word,
And put your trust in him with one accord.
For he hath evermore at hand,
His fountain's flow, his springs do never stand.
And plenteously he loveth to redeem,
Such sinners all,
As on him call,
And faithfully his mercies most esteem.

He will redeem our deadly drowning state,
He will bring home the sheep that go astray,
He will help them that hope in him alway:
He will appease our discord and debate,
He will soon save, though we repent us late.
He will be ours if we continue His,
He will bring bale to joy and perfect bliss.
He will redeem the flock of his elect,
From all that is,
Or was amiss.
Since Abraham's heirs did first his Law's reject.

Gascoigne's gardenings, written in one end of a close walk in his garden

The figure of this world I can compare,
To garden plots, and suchlike pleasant places,
The world breeds men of sundry shape and share,
As herbs in gardens, grow of sundry graces:
Some good, some bad, some amiable faces,
Some foul, some gentle, some of froward mind,
Subject like bloom, to blast of every wind.

And as you see the flowers most fresh of hue,
That they prove not always the wholesomest,
So fairest men are not always found true: 10
But even as withred weeds fall from the rest,
So flatterers fall naked from their nest:
When truth hath tried, their painting tising tale,
They lose their gloss, and all their jests seem stale.

Yet some do present pleasure most esteem,
Till beams of bravery wither all their wealth,
And some again there be can rightly deem,
Those herbs for best, which may maintain their health.
Considering well, that age draws on by stealth,
And when the fairest flower is shrunk and gone,   20
A well grown root, will stand and shift for one.

Then thus the restless life which men here lead,
May be resembled to the tender plant,
In spring it sprouts, as babes in cradle breed,
Flourish in May, like youths that wisdom want,
In autumn ripes and roots, lest store wax scant
In winter shrinks and shrouds from every blast,
Like crooked age when lusty youth is past.

And as the ground or grass whereon it grew,
Was fat or lean, even so by it appears   30
If barren soil, why then it changeth hue,
It fadeth fast, it flits to fumbling years,
But if he gathered root amongst his fears,
And light on land that was well muckte in deed,
Then stands it still, or leaves increase of seed.

As for the rest, fall sundry ways (God wot)
Some faint like froth at every little puff,
Some smart by sword, like herbs that serve the pot,
And some be weeded from the finer stuff,
Some stand by props to maintain all their ruff: 40
And thus (under correction be it told)
Hath Gascoigne gathered in his garden molde.

Haud ictus sapio

In that other end of his close walk, were written these toys in ryme.

If any flower that here is grown,
Or any herb may ease your pain,
Take and account it as your own,
But recompense the like again:
For some and some is honest play
And so my wife taught me to say.

If here to walk you take delight,
Why come, and welcome when you will:
If I bid you sup here this night,
Bid me another time, and still
Think some and some is honest play,
For so my wife taught me to say.

69

Thus if you sup or dine with me,
If you walk here, or sit at ease,
If you desire the thing you see,
And have the same your mind to please,
Think some and some is honest play,
And so my wife taught me to say.

Haud ictus sapio

In a chair in the same garden was written this

If thou sit here to view this pleasant garden place
Think thus: at last will come a frost, & all these flowers
deface:
But if thou sit at ease to rest thy weary bones,
Remember death brings final rest to all our grievous groans.
So whether for delight, or here thou sit for ease,
Think still upon the latter day, so shalt thou God best please.

Haud ictus sapio

Upon a stone in the wall of his garden he had written the year wherein he did the cost of these devises, and therewithall this posy in Latin

Quoniam etiam humiliatos, amœna delectant

70

The Tale of a Stone

An Epitaph upon Captaine Bourcher,
late slain in the wars in Zelande

Fie Captains fie, your tongues are tied too close,
Your soldiers eke by silence purchase shame:
Can no man pen in metre nor in prose,
The life, the death, the valiant acts, the fame,
The birth, behaviour, nor the noble name,
Of such a fear as you in fight have lost?
Alas such pains would quickly quite the cost.

Bourcher is dead, whom each of you did know,
Yet no man writes one word to paint his praise,
His sprite on high, his carcase here below,
Doth both condemn your doting idle days:
Yet cease they not to sound his worthy ways,
Who lived to die, and died again to live,
With death dear bought, he did his death forgive.

He might for birth have boasted noble race,
Yet were his manners meek and always mild,
Who gave a guess by gazing on his face,
And judged thereby, might quickly be beguiled,
In field a lion, and in town a child,
Fierce to his foe, but courteous to his friend.
Alas the while, his life so soon should end?

To serve his Prince his life was ever pressed,
To serve his God, his death he thought but dew,
In all attempts as forward as the best,
And all too forwards, which we all may rue,
His life so showed, his death eke tried it true:
For where his foes in thickest press did stand,

71

Bourcher caught bane with bloody sword in hand.

And mark the courage of a noble heart,
When he in bed lay wounded wondrous sore,
And heard alarm, he soon forgot his smart,
And called for arms to show his service more:
I will to field (quod he) and God before.
Which said, he sailed into more quiet coast,
Still praising God, and so gave up the ghost.

Now muse not reader though we stones can speak,
Or write sometimes the deeds of worthy ones,
I could not hold although my heart should break,
Because here by me buried are his bones,
But I must tell this tale thus for the nones
When men cry mumme and keep such silence long,
Then stones must speak, else dead men shall have wrong.

Certayne notes of Instruction
concerning the making of verse or ryme in English,
written at the request of Master Edouardo Donati.

Signor Edouardo, since promise is debt, and you (by the law of friendship) do burden me with a promise that I should lend you instructions towards the making of English verse or rhyme, I will assay to discharge the same, though not so perfectly as I would, yet as readily as I may: and therwithall I pray you consider that *Quot homines, tot Sententiæ*, especially in Poetry, wherein (nevertheless) I dare not challenge any degree, and yet will I at your request adventure to set down my simple skill in such simple manner as I have used, referring the same hereafter to the correction of the Laureate. And you shall have it in these few points following.

1 The first and most necessary point that ever I found meet to be considered in making of a delectable poem is this, to ground it upon some fine invention. For it is not enough to roll in pleasant words, nor yet to thunder in *Rhyme, Ram, Ruff,* by letter (quoth my master Chaucer) nor yet to abound in apt vocables, or epithets, unless the invention have in it also *aliquid salis*. By this *aliquid salis*, I mean some good and fine devise, showing the quick capacity of a writer: and where I say some good and fine invention, I mean that I would have it both fine and good. For many inventions are so superfine, that they are *Vix* good. And again many Inventions are good, and yet not finely handled. And for a general forewarning: what theme soever you do take in hand, if you do handle it but *tanquam in oratione perpetua*, and never study for some depth of devise in the Invention, & some figures also in the handling thereof: it will appear to the skilful reader but a tale of a tub. To deliver unto you general examples it were almost unpossible, since the occasions of Inventions are (as it were) infinite: nevertheless take in worth mine opinion, and perceive my further meaning in these few points. If I should undertake to write in praise of a gentlewoman, I would neither praise her crystal eye, nor her cherry lip, &c. For these things are *trita & obvia*. But I would either find some supernatural cause whereby my pen might walk in the superlative degree, or else I would undertake to answer for any imperfection that she hath, and thereupon raise the praise of her commendation. Likewise if I should disclose my pretence in love, I would either make a strange discourse of some intolerable passion, or find occasion to plead by the example of some history, or discover my disquiet in shadows *per Allegoriam*, or use the covertest means that I could to avoid the uncomely customs of common writers. Thus much I adventure to deliver unto you (my friend) upon the rule of Invention, which of all other rules is most to be marked, and hardest to be prescribed in certain and infallible rules, nevertheless to conclude therein, I would have you stand most upon the excellency of your Invention, & stick not to study deeply for some fine devise. For that being found, pleasant words will follow well enough and fast enough.

2 Your Invention being once devised, take heed that neither pleasure of rhyme, nor variety of devise, do carry you from it: for as to use obscure & dark phrases in a pleasant sonnet, is nothing delectable, so to intermingle merry jests in a serious matter is an indecorum.

3 I will next advise you that you hold the just measure wherewith you begin your verse, I will not deny but this may seem a preposterous order: but because I covet rather to satisfy you particularly, than to undertake a general tradition,

I will not so much stand upon the manner as the matter of my precepts. I say then, remember to hold the same measure wherewith you begin, whether it be in a verse of six syllables, eight, ten, twelve, &c. and though this precept might seem ridiculous unto you, since every young scholar can conceive that he ought to continue in the same measure wherewith he beginneth, yet do I see and read many men's poems nowadays, which beginning with the measure of xii. in the first line, & xiiii. in the second (which is the common kind of verse) they will yet (by that time they have passed over a few verses) fall into xiiii. & fourteen, & *sic de similibus*, the which is either forgetfulness or carelessness.

4 And in your verses remember to place every word in his natural emphasis or sound, that is to say in such wise, and with such length or shortness, elevation or depression of syllables, as it is commonly pronounced or used: to express the same we have three manner of accents, *gravis, le[v]is*, & *circumflexa*, the which I would English thus, the long accent, the short accent, & that which is indifferent: the grave accent is marked by this character, / the light accent is noted thus, \ & the circumflex or indifferent is thus signified ~: the grave accent is drawn out or elevated, and maketh that syllable long whereupon it is placed: the light accent is depressed or snatched up, and maketh that syllable short upon the which it lighteth: the circumflex accent is indifferent, sometimes short, sometimes long, sometimes depressed & sometimes elevated. For example of the emphasis or natural sound of words, this word **treasure** hath the grave accent upon the first syllable, whereas if it should be written in this sort, **treasúre**, now were the second syllable long, & that were clean contrary to the common use wherewith it is pronounced. For further explanation hereof, note you that commonly nowadays in English rhymes (for I dare not call them English verses) we use none other order

75

but a foot of two syllables, whereof the first is depressed or made short, & the second is elevated or made long: and that sound or scanning continues throughout the verse. We have used in times past other kinds of metres: as for example this following:

No wight in this world, that wealth can attayne,
\ /   \ \ /   \ / \ \ /
Unless he believe, that all is but vain

Also our father Chaucer has used the same liberty in feet and measures that the Latinists do use: and whosoever peruses and well considers his works, shall find that although his lines are not always of one selfsame number of syllables, yet being read by one that has understanding, the longest verse and that which has most syllables in it, will fall (to the ear) correspondent unto that which hath fewest syllables in it: and likewise that which has in it fewest syllables, shall be found yet to consist of words that have such natural sound, as may seem equal in length to a verse which has many more syllables of lighter accents. And surely I can lament that we are fallen into such a plain and simple manner of writing, that there is no other foot used but one: wherby our Poems may justly be called Rhythms, and cannot by any right challenge the name of a Verse. But since it is so, let us take the ford as we find it, and let me set down unto you such rules or precepts that even in this plain foot of two syllables you wrest no word from his natural and usual sound, I do not mean hereby that you may use no other words but of two syllables, for therein you may use discretion according to occasion of matter: but my meaning is, that all the words in your verse be so placed as the first syllable may sound short or be depressed, the second long or elevated, the third short, the fourth long, the fifth short, &c. For example of my meaning in this point mark these two verses:

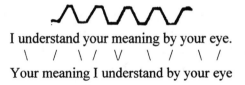

I understand your meaning by your eye.
\ / \ / V \ / \ /
Your meaning I understand by your eye

In these two verses there seems no difference at all, since one has the very selfsame words that the other has, and yet the latter verse is neither true nor pleasant, & the first verse may pass muster. The fault of the latter verse is that this word **understand** is therein so placed as the grave accent falls upon **der**, and thereby makes **der**, in this word **understand** to be elevated: which is contrary to the natural or usual pronunciation: for we say

\ \ / \ / \
under**stand**, and not under**stand**.

5 Here by the way I think it not amiss to forewarn you that you thrust as few words of many syllables into your verse as may be: and hereunto I might allege many reasons: first the most ancient English words are of one syllable, so that the more monosyllables that you use, the truer Englishman you shall seem, and the less you shall smell of the inkhorn.

Also words of many syllables do cloy a verse and make it unpleasant, whereas words of one syllable will more easily fall to be short or long as occasion requires, or will be adapted to become circumflex or of an indifferent sound.

6 I would exhort you also to beware of rhyme without reason: my meaning is hereby that your rhyme lead you not from your first invention, for many writers when they have laid the platform of their invention, are yet drawn sometimes (by rhyme) to forget it or at least to alter it, as when they cannot readily find out a word which may rhyme to the first (and yet continue their determinate invention) they do then either botch it up with a word that will rhyme (how small reason soever it carry with it) or else they alter their first word and so percase decline or trouble their former invention: But do you always hold your first determined invention, and do rather search the bottom of your brains for apt words, than change good reason for rumbling rhyme.

7   To help you a little with rhyme (which is also a plain young scholar's lesson) work thus, when you have set down your first verse, take the last word thereof and count over all the words of the selfsame sound by order of the alphabet: As for example, the last word of your first line is **care**, to rhyme therewith you have **bare**, **clare**, **dare**, **fare**, **gare**, **hare**, and **share**, **mare**, **snare**, **rare**, **stare**, & **ware**, &c. Of all these take that which best may serve your purpose, carrying reason with rhyme: and if none of them will serve so, then alter the last word of your former verse, but yet do not willingly alter the meaning of your invention.

8   You may use the same figures or tropes in verse which are used in prose, and in my judgement they serve more aptly, and have greater grace in verse than they have in prose: but yet therein remember this old adage, *Ne quid nimis*, as many writers which do not know the use of any other figure than that which is expressed in repetition of sundry words beginning all with one letter, the which (being modestly used) lends good grace to a verse: but they do so hunt a letter to death, that they make it *Crambé*, and *Crambe his positum mors est*: therefore *Ne quid nimis*.

9   Also as much as may be, eschew strange words, or *obsoleta & inusitata*, unless the theme do give just occasion: marie in some places a strange word doth draw attentive

reading, but yet I would have you therein to use discretion.

10 And as much as you may, frame your style to perspicuity and to be sensible: for the haughty obscure verse doth not much delight, and the verse that is too easy is like a tale of a roasted horse: but let your poem be such as may both delight and draw attentive reading, and therewithal may deliver such matter as be worth the marking.

11 You shall do very well to use your verse after the English phrase, and not after the manner of other languages: The Latinists commonly set the adjective after the substantive: As for example *Femina pulchra, œdes altœ*, &c. but if we should say in English *a woman fair, a house high*, &c. it would have but small grace: for we say *a good man*, and not *a man good*, &c. And yet I will not altogether forbid it you, for in some places, it may be borne, but not so hardly as some use it which write thus:

> Now let us go to temple ours,
> I will go visit mother mine &c.

Surely I smile at the simplicity of such devisers which might as well have said it in plain English phrase, and yet have better pleased all ears, than they satisfy their own fancies by such *superfinesse*. Therefore even as I have advised you to place all words in their natural or most common and usual pronunciation, so would I wish you to frame all sentences in their mother phrase and proper *Idióma*, and yet sometimes (as I have said before) the contrary may be borne, but that is rather where rhyme enforceth, or *per licentiam Poëticam*, than it is otherwise lawful or commendable.

12 This poetical licence is a shrewd fellow, and covers many faults in a verse. It makes words longer, shorter, of more syllables, of fewer, newer, older, truer, falser, and to conclude it turkeneth all things at pleasure, for example, *ydone* for *done*, *adowne* for *downe*, *orecome* for *overcome*, *tane* for *taken*, *power* for *powre*, *heaven* for *heavn*, *thewes* for *good parts* or *good qualities*, and a number of others which it were but tedious and needless to rehearse, since your own judgement and reading will soon make you espy such advantages.

13 There are also certain pauses or rests in a verse which may be called Ceasures, whereof I would be loth to stand long, since it is at discretion of the writer, and they have been first devised (as should seem) by the musicians: but yet thus much I will adventure to write, that in my opinion in a verse of eight syllables, the pause will stand best in the middest, in a verse of ten it will best be placed at the end of the first four syllables: in a verse of twelve, in the midst, in verses of twelve, in the first and fourteen in the second, we place the pause commonly in the midst of the first, and at the end of the first eight syllables in the second. In rhythm royal, it is at the writer's discretion, and forceth not where the pause be until the end of the line.

14 And here because I have named rhythm royal, I will tell you also my opinion as well of that as of the names which other rhymes have commonly borne heretofore. Rhythm royal is a verse of ten syllables, and seven such verses make a staff, whereof the first and third lines do answer (across) in like terminations and rhyme, the second, fourth, and fifth, do likewise answer each other in terminations, and the two last do combine and shut up the sentence: this has been called rhythm royal, & surely it is a royal kind of verse, serving best for grave discourses. There is also another kind called Ballad, and thereof are sundry sorts: for a man may write ballad in a staff of six lines, every line containing eight or six syllables, whereof the first and third, second and fourth do rhyme across, and the fifth and sixth do rhyme together in

80

conclusion. You may write also your ballad of ten syllables rhyming as before is declared, but these two were wont to be most commonly used in ballad, which proper name was (I think) derived of this word in Italian *Ballare*, which signifies *to dance*. And indeed those kinds of rhymes serve best for dances or light matters. Then have you also a rondlette, the which doth always end with one selfsame foot or repetition, and was thereof (in my judgement) called *a rondelet*. This may consist of such measure as best liketh the writer, then have you sonnets, some think that all poems (being short) may be called sonnets, as indeed it is a diminutive word derived of *Sonare*, but yet I can best allow to call those sonnets which are of fourteen lines, every line containing ten syllables. The first twelve do rhyme in staves of four lines by cross metre, and the last two rhyming together do conclude the whole. There are Dyzaynes, & Syxaines which are of ten lines, and of six lines, commonly used by the French, which some English writers do also term by the name of sonnets. Then is there an old kind of rhyhm called Verlayes, derived (as I have read) of this word *Verd* which betokeneth *green*, and *Laye* which betokeneth *a song*, as if you would say *green songs*: but I must tell you by the way, that I never read any verse which I saw by authority called *Verlay*, but one, and that was a long discourse in verses of ten syllables, whereof the four first did rhyme across, and the fifth did answer to the first and third, breaking off there, and so going on to another termination. Of this I could show example of imitation in my own verses written to the right honourable the Lord Grey of Wilton, "Gascoigne's Voyage into Holland in 1572", &c. There are also certain poems devised of ten syllables, whereof the first answers in termination with the fourth, and the second and third answer each other: these are more used by other nations than by us, neither can I tell readily what name to give them. And the commonest sort of verse which we use nowadays (*viz.* the long verse of twelve and fourteen syllables) I know not certainly how to name it, unless I should say that it consists of Poulter's measure, which gives twelve for one dozen and fourteen for another. But let this suffice (if it be not too much) for the sundry sorts of verses which we use nowadays.

15 In all these sorts of verses when soever you undertake to write, avoid prolixity and tediousness, & ever as near as you can, do finish the sentence and meaning at the end of every staff where you write staves, & at the end of every two lines where you write by cooples or Poulter's measure: for I see many writers which draw their sentences in length, & make an end at latter Lammas: for commonly before they end, the reader hath forgotten where he began. But do you (if you will follow my advice) eschew prolixity and knit up your sentences as compendiously as you may, since brevity (so that it be not drowned in obscurity) is most commendable.

16 I had forgotten a notable kind of rhyme, called riding rhyme, and that is such as our master and father Chaucer used in his *Canterbury Tales*, and in diverse other delectable and light enterprises: but though it has come to my remembrance somewhat out of order, it shall not yet come altogether out of time, for I will now tell you a conceit which I had before forgotten to write: you may see (by the way) that I hold a preposterous order in my traditions, but as I said before I write moved by good will, and not to show my skill. Then to return to my matter, as this riding rhyme serves most aptly to write a merry tale, so rhythm royal is fittest for a grave discourse. Ballads are best of matters of love, and rondlettes most apt for the beating or handling of an adage or common proverb: sonnets serve as well in matters of love as of discourse: Dyzaynes and Syxaines for short fantasies: Verlayes for an effectual proposition,

82

although by the name you might otherwise judge of Verlayes, and the long verse of twelve and fourteen syllables, although it be nowadays used in all themes, yet in my judgement it would serve best for psalms and hymns.

I would stand longer in these traditions, were it not that I doubt mine own ignorance, but as I said before, I know that I write to my friend, and affying myself thereupon, I make an end.

FINIS

Notes to "Certayne notes of Instruction concerning the making of verse or ryme in English"

Master Edouardo Donati an unidentified acquaintance of Gascoigne's
Quot homines, tot Sententiæ as many men, so many opinions
(1) **Chaucer** a quotation from the Prologue to *The Parson's Tale* in which Chaucer mocks heavily alliterative verse
aliquid salis some wit
tanquam in oratione perpetua as if in a perpetual speech
trita & obvia well worn and ready to hand
(3) *sic de similibus* and the same is true in similar cases
(8) *Ne quid nimis* nothing to excess
Crambe his positum mors est cabbage placed in these matters is death (possibly an allusion to Juvenal's description of hackneyed repetition as "twice cooked cabbage" [*Satires*, 7, line 154])
(9) *obsoleta & inusitata* obsolete and uncommon
(12) **turkeneth** twists
(14) **Poulter's measure** a metre consisting of lines of 12 and 14 syllables alternately
(15) **cooples** couplets
latter Lammas a day that will never come
16) **affying** daring to trust

83

NOTES TO THE POEMS

Notes followed by a (G) indicate original annotations by Gascoigne.

In Praise of the Brown Beauty (p. 11)
5 **gite** gown
6 **tysing** enticing **Pallas** the goddess Pallas Athene; possibly also playing on "palace"
9 **eld** old age
12 **tickle** easily fooled or excited

When First I Thee Beheld (p. 12)
1 **black and white** symbolizing a commitment to lifelong virginity
15 **guerdon** reward

The Praise of Phillip Sparrow (p.13)
Sparrow in Latin a synonym for penis
15 **lays on load** sings for all she is worth
23 **fend cut** a defensive fencing stroke
24 **peat** a spoiled or pampered girl
26 **proyned** preened
39 **by-the-rood** by the cross [of Christ]

Soon Acquainted, Soon Forgotten (p. 15)
7 **recule** recoil
9 **Cresside** Gascoigne is alluding to Chaucer's long narrative poem *Troilus and Criseyde*
10 **freamed cheare** wild (or unfamiliar) cheer

A Lover Often Warned (p. 16)
28 **cates** the best and daintiest food

Gascoigne's Passion (p. 19)
43 **the fever Ectyck** "There is in deede suche a kinde of fever" (G)
60 **past** surpasses all others

A Hundreth Suns (p. 22)
7 **The youngest sister** Atropos, one of three fatal sisters, was the fate that ends man's life [see Note to "The Feeble Thread" below]

Gascoigne's Libel of Divorce (p. 23)
12 **he that bears the bell** the best or most excellent
21 **lemman** mistress

You Must Not Wonder (p. 24)
6 **tysed** tempted
14 **bale** funeral pyre or destruction

Gascoigne's Recantation (p. 25)
28 **my tippet here I turn** I turn traitor
32 **Astolf** The tale of Astolf's queen's sex romps with a dwarf is told in Canto 28 of Ariosto's *Orlando Furioso*

Either a Needless or a Bootless Comparison Between Two Letters (p. 26)
1 **the christ's cross row** the alphabet (the cross row was a child's teaching aid)
4 *A. O. G. N. C. S.* ie. GASCON, or Gascoigne

The Feeble Thread (p. 34)
1 *Lachesis* like *Atropos* (6) one of the three fates in classical mythology. Lachesis spins the thread of life, Clotho holds the spindle and Atropus cuts the thread. There is an encounter with them in Spenser's *Faerie Queene*, Book 4, Canto 2, stanzas 47-52.

85

4 **wale** texture
15 **slipper** having a smooth, slippery surface

**Counsel given to master Bartholmew Withipoll
a little before his latter journey to Geane, 1572**   (p. 36)
Bartholmew Withipoll a close friend of Gascoigne's
Geane Genoa
1 **Bat** like **Batte** a friendly abbreviation of "Bartholomew"
14 **geazon** extraordinary or amazing
43 **peason** something of very small value or importance
46 *Da, da*, **sir** *K* "Yes, yes, sir knight"
49 **the foolish blink-eyed boy** a private reference to
something known only to Gascoigne and his friend
Bartholomew; Gascoigne appends a marginal note to the
next line with the deadpan comment: "A Misterie."
51 **toy** youth or plaything
69 **thou comest for the shells of Christ** you are on a
pilgrimage [the scallop shell, originally associated with the
pilgrimage to Compostela and the shrine of St James, was
the symbol or badge of the pilgrim]
72 *Magnifico* Lord
73 *fico* fig
78 **Spanish soap** a type of fine soap made with olive-oil
and soda
84 **buskins** boots
88 **doublet** sleeved waistcoat **Bumbaste** padding
96 **for the nones** for the occasion
107 **piketooth** toothpick
109 **Coptanckt** a high-crowned hat shaped like a sugar-loaf
111 **sloppe** fashionable baggy trousers (a "slender" sloppe is
an absurd contradiction, invoking the ridiculousness of
foreign fashion) **docke** buttocks
112 **curtold** short
114 **like** *Marquise of all Beef* like a pompous idiot
115 **spilt** wasted

118 **My hindmost *P*** ie. the Pox, or venereal disease, but also punningly alluding to piles

126 **Spanish buttons** scabs

131 **Guido** unidentified but presumably a doctor specialising in the treatment of venereal disease

146 **Pencoyde** Sir William Morgan of Pencoyde

147 **James a Parrye** unidentified

150 **the Spa** Spa (now in Belgium) was the first town to become popular for the health-giving qualities of its mineral springs. Henry VIII went there.

154 **in gree** with favour

Despised Things May Live (p. 43)

10 **shrich** screech

11 **set full light** disdained

14 **playne** lament

27 **recure** recovery

Magnum vectigal parcimonia (p. 45)

This title literally means "a great tax is frugality" and is a quotation from Cicero's *Paradoxes of the Stoics*, 6.3.49.

2-3 **a bottle... a wallet** items carried by a beggar or vagrant

4 **bravery** such fine clothes as a beggar's

12 **Hick, Hobbe, and Dick** any common person (ie. the Elizabethan equivalent of "any Tom, Dick or Harry")

13 **goonhole groats** small change (a groat was worth two pence)

15 **let their lease and took their rent before** sold a lease for cash and received advance payment for rent

16 **raps a royal on his cap** pays in gold coins for his hat

18 **broach a better tap** find a better way

23 **old angels** gold coins portraying the archangel Michael spearing a dragon; they were worth about ten shillings

26 **haggard hawks mislike an empty hand** adult hawks

spurn a hand without a lure
30 **Davie Debet**   debt or poverty
32 **like**   regard
37 **Malmesey**   a sweet wine
42 **hooches**   chests
Sic tuli. "this is how I have translated it" (referring to the title)

Gascoigne's Woodmanship   (p. 47)

1 **My worthy Lord**   Arthur, Lord Grey of Wilton, later a patron of Edmund Spenser and notorious after Gascoigne's death for his role in the 1580 massacre of civilians and surrendered soldiers at Smerwick in Ireland. Spenser saw him as "most gentle, affable, loving, and temperate" but acknowledged that his detractors called him "a bloody man"
2 **your woodman**   ie. Gascoigne himself
3 **a sot**   a drunkard or fool
5 **carren**   a doe with young (unfit for eating)
7 **barren**   a doe neither pregnant nor with young
8 **hap**   luck
22 **Littleton**   author of a well-known law book
23 **a daw**   a simpleton
25 **Fitzherbert**   author of a major law treatise
25-26 **such a brain, / As Tully had, to write the law by art**   Cicero (Marcus Tullius Cicero) was usually known as Tully at this time. Cicero wrote a treatise on the law.
31 **He winked wrong**   He sighted his bow incorrectly
45 **fleareth**   smiles ingratiatingly and mockingly
50 **begarded all with gay**   brightly decorated
53 **Peter pence**   slang for a bribe
67 **Flushing frays**   an allusion to Gascoigne's recent military service in the Low Countries. Flushing (nowadays known as Vlissingen) is a Dutch port
75 **sakeless**   guiltless
78 **And shear him out his share...**   And pay him in rags

81 **pull the spoil from such as pill**   pillage
96 **on the molde** on earth
100 **prick** in archery, the wooden peg at the target's centre
105 **Old Parkins, Rastall, and Dan Bracten's books**
well-known contemporary legal treatises
109 **maw** mouth
139 **sodaine** suddenness

Gascoigne's Voyage to Holland in 1572 (p. 52)

5 *Alderlievest*   best beloved (G)
10 **pastaunce** pastime
12 *en bon gré*   in good worth (G)
18 **starting hole** hiding place
20 **welkin** sky
25 **gauld** chaffed until raw and painful
28 **ranging** sweeping and lengthy
34 **Quinborough** Queenborough, a port on the Isle of
Sheppey, at the mouth of the Thames estuary
42 **A ferly chaunce** A strange trick of fate
62 **Aloof, aloof** Turn the helm to windward
66 **And went to Hull** Not the town but a nautical
expression meaning "When all sayles are taken downe" (G)
70 **a swadde** a lout or fool
71 **tone** possibly "tun" or barrell
72 *Ghy zijt te vroegh* "You be too soon" (G)
73 *Tis niet goet tijt*   "It is not good tide" (G)
81 **Alba** The Duke of Alva, commander of the Spanish
troops fighting against the Dutch and their English allies
87 **wond** navigated the ship
89 **pilot's craft**   in the original "*Pylats* crafte", alluding to
the cunning of Pontius Pilate (see Matthew, Ch. 27)
94 **run on head** act rashly
101 **Daunsk** Danzig
102 **Frize** Friesland
105 **Breyll** Brielle, a Dutch port

107 **uncouth** "unknown" (G)

109 **a gospel on that mouth** a blessing on those words

111 **the sowne** the depth

120 *Die tijt is goet, dat heb ick weell bekend.* "It is good tide that know I well" (G)

127 **the hundred and seventh Psalm** Gascoigne presumably had in mind verses 23 - 30.

132 *Edell Bloetts* "Lusty gallants" (G)

139 **fleet and flow** drift

142 **swage** assuage

143 **selly** helpless **sowst** drenched

150 **blinne** remain

169 **engrave** strongly influence

201 **pestred** crowded

203 **My chief companions** "Yorke and Herle" (G), Rowland Yorke and William Herle, both probably involved with Walsingham's intelligence service

227 **bowge** split open

231 **a hoy** small sailing ship used to carry goods over short distances

238 **carke** care (G)

255 **mysease** affliction

277 **trulls** whores

280 **clink** prison

283 **pynke** "A Small bote" (G)

292 **Bulbeef** tough, poor quality meat

296 **buttered beer** a sweet, rich beer containing sugar, cinnamon and butter, brewed without hops

297 **sops of browesse** broth made from leftovers

301 **Haarlem** The siege of Haarlem began on 11 December, 1572

336 *met v*: and *anders niet* with you and not with others

344 **John Zuche** evidently, like **Ned Dennye**, a former aquaintance of Gascoigne's

349 **master Moyle** Sir Thomas Moyle, Speaker of the

House of Commons under Henry VII and a famous hunter of heretics

The Green Knight's Farewell to Fancy (p. 62)
40 **burdens** bourdons (the lowest bell in a peal of bells)
45 **water boughs** undergrowth
47 **griffe** graft   **pippin** young apple tree

Gascoigne's De Profundis (p. 65)
De Profundis A quotation from Psalm 129 Verse One in the Latin Bible: *De profundis clamavi ad te Domine* (translated in the Authorised Version, where it is Psalm 130, as "Out of the depths have I cried unto thee O Lord").
18 **in ure** into practice
49 **attendeth** waits

Gascoigne's gardenings, written in one end of a close walk in his garden (p. 68)
3 **share** type
13 **tising** enticing
16 **bravery** extravagance
34 **muckte** manured
40 **ruff** finery (with a play on the ruff worn around the neck, which was sometimes supported by wire)
42 **molde** earth
Quoniam etiam humiliatos, amœna delectant For pleasant things delight even those who have been humbled

The Tale of a Stone (p. 71)
The narrator of this poem is Bourcher's gravestone; it ends with a "posy" stating "Finis quod Marmaduke Marblestone"
Captain Bourcher Captain Bourcher was killed in 1573 near Middelburg